The Way to

Economic Suicide of the United States

A Blueprint that Would Help to Avoid it

The Way to

Economic Suicide of the United States

a Blueprint that Would Help Avoid it

Robert A. Peterson

Lulu Enterprises, Inc.

Peterson, Robert A., 1925–
        The Way to Economic Suicide of the United States: A Blueprint
that Would Help Avoid it / Robert A. Peterson

Includes bibliographical references.
ISBN: 978-0-557-90888-2
1.   Business & Economics/ Government & Business.   2.   Political Science / Economic Conditions

Cover art adapted from etchings by J. J. Grandville.
Compliments to David Gothard for his illustration in
the July 15, 2010 *WSJ*, which, though similar, was not a
known inspiration for this cover illustration.

Book Design by Alcuin Communications, LLC, Tucson, Arizona

Contents

Introduction

The following is an examination of the deterioration of the economic activity in the United States, its root cause and those practices that enhance the down turn

President Obama has frequently said he inherited this mess, which has some element of truth. However, he inherited it from President Carter, the author of the Community Development Act, and President Clinton whose administration put in rules and penalties to the banks that gave them little choice but to take on excessive risks. In addition, HUD increased the amount of risky loans required and Freddie Mac and Fannie Mae acquiesced to these coercions. Senator Obama joined with his Democratic colleagues to sustain the filibuster of the 2005 McCain Bill to regulate Fannie and Freddie. Additionally the Democrats became the majority party in 2006 and did not pursue regulations for Freddie and Fannie. The risks increased when President Clinton signed the bill that rescinded the Glass-Steagall Act that previously prevented Banks from also being an investment bank and permitted the risks they subsequently took.

The legislation action, such as the Stimulus Bill, added to the current push for a carbon tax, plus a new Healthcare Bill, which under both the House and Senate versions result in massive tax and fee increase and will result in lower economic activity. The result will be decreased tax revenues. The forgoing, combined with additional spending, equals ballooning deficits. It is hoped this does not result in the financial pandemic that appears likely.

The damage being done to the liberty of this republic in the name of needed changes for the economy to recover, cannot be ignored and would show:

- The federal government now has control of the banking system and may determine who gets borrowed funds and who does not.

- The federal government has control of the mortgage market and may determine who gets mortgages and who does not.

- The U.S. Government now controls student loans with no outside source of these loans. As a result the government may determine who gets loans to go to college and universities and who does not.

- The federal government has taken over two of the big three automobile manufacturers and with imposed mileage standards (generally referred to as café standards) is mandating what cars the public can buy.

Nowhere is there a more illogical conclusion that jobs and cheap power will result from so called green energy. Economic professor Arthur Upgren once said, "it isn't what you know that hurts you, it's what you know that isn't so." Roger Meiners' article "Talking Green in Yellowstone" (in the *Wall Street Journal* August 21-22, 2010 edition) reports Ennis National Fish Hatchery, U.S. Fish & Wildlife Service received $179,000 in stimulus money to install solar panels that will replace $2,550 in annual electrical power costs. Angel Gonzalez and Keith Johnson's article in the *Wall Street Journal*, dated September 3, 2010, "Spain's Solar Power Collapse Dims Subsidy Model" reflects on how "the Spanish Government slammed the brakes on generous subsidies."

If the Carbon Tax goes through, the means of producing electricity will bear large increases in these taxes, which will result in large increases in electrical and other energy costs to the consumer. The government's direction, in energy production toward so-called green energy will almost surely lead to electricity shortages and its rationing. Saddam Hussein used the cutoff of electricity to control the populace.

In the past, the print media and the evening newscast would have examined many of these policies in detail and reported on them. Today we have de facto censorship where the media doesn't report news that doesn't fit their political agenda. The government announced they would fully guarantee the obligations of Freddie and Fannie, on

Christmas Eve, yet there was almost no mention of this in the media or investigation about it in subsequent editions. For whatever reason, these traditional sources of investigative journalism have abdicated their role. Similarly political correctness infringes on free speech. Where does this originate it? Who decides what is proper and what is not? A guess would be that it's the same media.

No matter which party is in power, the foregoing is a danger to our liberties if abused by someone who would use them for their own purposes.

In our formation, the colonists tired of King George III and the rest of the royal family who took resources of their subjects as their right. The colonists threw off this ruling elite by forming the United States. How is it different from King George III where the spending and taxing bills are being rammed through Congress? The United States is supposed to be a representative democracy. How is this so when every poll shows it is not what the large majority of Americans want?

The foregoing and the following are the author's opinion, which grew from his background, information shared by others, and his understanding of arithmetic. Where pertinent, the chapter will show where the reader can review others' thoughts on these same subjects and draw their own conclusions. There are also some paths of different direction that the reader and others may agree holds promise.

ONE

The Cause Of The Economic Downturn

Congress Lights the Fuse

The root cause of the economic downturn was the program to sell houses to people who couldn't pay for them and the push to build affordable housing that resulted in every community doing so in the form of tract condos and townhouses that are not suitable for the elderly. Those responsible are those who pushed these programs. They include but are not limited to, Jimmy Carter, who arrived at the concept and got legislation passed for "the Community Development Act," the Clinton administration believed in the act. Acorn and other similar organizations filed lawsuits (the most notable was against Citibank). In this case, a judge ruled that credit standards had to be lowered to accommodate those who did not reach the standards other borrowers had to achieve.

Senior members of the House and Senate, joined by other advocacy groups armed with the judicial ruling, appeared to intimidate the banks and other lending institutions, which resulted in the banks being aggressive in taking on these loans. Two of the most visible exponents were in the House, Barney Frank and in the Senate, Chris Dodd. This was further compounded with Fannie Mae and Freddie Mac aggressively buying up these mortgages. In some cases – it is rumored – the broker at "Countrywide Finance" was urged to upgrade his analysis of credit worthiness with the commitment that these two institutions would buy the mortgage. Recently, some of those who purchased these mortgages were preparing legal action, alleging incomes of the borrowers were not verified, as well as other pertinent data.

To arrive at a payment amount that the borrower felt they could handle, they permitted the mortgage to start out at a rate that only the best credits were given. This was done for a short period of time (a couple of years), at which point the rate was scheduled to increase to a level that reflected the normal rate they would have qualified for. Another way of keeping the original payment down was to use an adjustable rate mortgage (ARM), so that as the market rates rose, the payment amount increased to a point where it could not be met by the borrower.

Another dirty little secret is the federal government's unfunded mandates to the states; the state government passes these mandates to the counties. The county government passes these on to the cities and other local governments and then to the homeowners that has skyrocketed the cost of taxes on real estate that have nothing to do with local services. This should be stopped; it effectively dictates federal government mandates to all of the state and local governments and it results in taxes on the local entities being imposed by the federal government. It is not unusual for these taxes to be a third of the required monthly payment. A law should be passed that these mandates can be refused and those that are put into effect be paid in full by the federal government and when they quit funding them the program stops. The funding should also include their portion of the fixed costs that are used. The housing price bubble drove assessed valuations higher and local governments are using every stalling idea to avoid reducing them.

As it became apparent that there was a glut of housing, the prices began to fall. Those homeowners who had little or no equity in their house realized they would be better off economically walking away from their mortgage. This was also encouraged by the drive up of local taxes that made their payments more difficult. This drove prices down even further, which hurt the homeowners who had played by the rules. Most people considered the equity in their house as savings. As the values began to fall they have pulled back from their spending and started to save money to replace the valuations in their home that they have lost.

Look no further for the trigger of the recession. It is the United States Congress and Senate who pushed this legislation that resulted in selling homes to people who couldn't afford to pay for them. Those who pushed our country into this madness are responsible. It is strange that the economic downturn, which is variously described as the worst since the great depression, isn't under investigation by an independent panel to find out what caused it.

Members of Congress, officials at HUD and management of Freddie-Fannie, know they created the environment for this mess. To divert attention from the government's involvement, legislative hearings were held where others were berated for making these bad loans. It's the most unkind cut of all that those who literally forced the banks to make these loans are the ones criticizing them now.

With this history, you would have thought they learned their lesson. Barney Frank and his crew are thinking of new ways to reduce the payments including forgiving parts of the loan.

This downward spiral in home valuations must be stopped. However, with the current direction of the Administration and Congress, it is feared will create the same dismal results.

There are different family classes affected by the failed policies of the Community Development Act:

- There are those who are working and are stressed in their financing because of losses in value of their property due to the downturn in home values.

- There are those who have lost their job and have been prudent in their financing and life style in the past;

- There are also those who never had the resources to own their own home and have little prospect of doing so in the future.

Some ways to reduce the pressure on the groups and as a result reduce the pressure on the housing market:

- Those in the first group are making their payments on time and don't have plans to sell their house. Even so it appears that they fear any change in their jobs would put them in difficult circumstances. A likely result may be a less spending mentality replaced by cash conservation one. This is the largest homeowner group. Their change to a more positive attitude would reap great economic benefits to the United States. There is a need to increase the cash resources of this group, which would provide cash flow, some would pay off credit cards, and others would increase their spending. The results may be an upbeat mentality in these homeowners and will likely reduce the homes going onto the market. The government should not be the source of this cash, as it would further increase the national debt. As the banks Freddie and Fanny participated in creating the housing problems their help in solving it should be required. Banks should offer the first group, a three-year moratorium on the payment of the principle of the mortgage. This is the payment portion scheduled to pay down the mortgage. This action would result in a balloon payment at the end of the mortgage, or the term would be extended for three years. This would keep the money in the hands of the homeowner. The incentive for the banks is to have the regulators and auditors agree that for book and performance requirements that they will account them as good assets. It would also be acknowledgment of their role in creating this mess.

- To alleviate the fear of losing their home on those who have always been employed but have lost their jobs, a program that gives them time to adjust to their dilemma through retraining or other activities would qualify them for up to a three year non-principal payment program. The federal government would also pay, for up to an eighteen-month period, interest, real estate taxes, house insurance and medical insurance so that they had time to orderly sell their house or adjust their life needs.

- The money for this program would come from the Stimulus Bill in place of planting trees in the Amazon, protecting the fuzzy mouse and other pet projects of little importance.

- The third group cannot and have not been able to own a house and some program needs to be put in place to help them get into rental space and unburden them of the crushing debt of house payments, taxes, insurance and maintenance required in home ownership. To dispose of the properties, in default, set up a "Resolution Trust," similar to the one used during the savings and loan crisis.

One of the groups that could be potential buyers for these homes and subsequently be landlords are the unemployed construction workers who have the skills necessary to maintain these properties through their sweat equity. They would need the following help from the federal government:

- Where there are laws that prevent eviction for nonpayment of the rent, change the law.

- Eliminate the laws that prevent a delay in eviction for non-payment of rent. Similarly, get rid of the restriction for discontinuing gas or electric service for nonpayment. Where compassion is in order, these payments are to be the responsibility of the governmental unit ordering that the utility and the landlord not enforce their right.

- Additionally those who do not treat the property with respect need to become part of a register and the landlord can refuse to rent to those who have a history of trashing rental property.

- Additionally, the new landlords would need attractive mortgage financing and rudimentary accounting and business training.

The foregoing would make available good structurally maintained rental housing. These lower income people are entitled to lodging that are decent places to live. This would not occur without addressing the crime and gang problems. The sale of illegal drugs provides the income for these criminals to exist.

This does not suggest that drugs should be legalized. The reality is that marijuana has been effectually legalized. The approval by many states of medical marijuana, coupled with the federal drug enforcement decision to not prosecute marijuana sale is tantamount to legalization. There is also massive growing of marijuana in our national parks. Why not recognize that this is true and put the government in control of its production and sale through drug store outlets to adults? In every case the drug store price must be significantly lower than the street price and with severe penalties imposed for those selling to the under age. Under such a program, the same penalties would apply as it does for alcohol such as driving under the influence, etc. This would dry up an enormous cash flow to this criminal element, helping to clean up crime in the neighborhoods and would certainly help our Mexican neighbors' efforts in controlling the drug cartels. In no way does this endorse the use of marijuana, but does recognize the problems of the criminal element it creates. Our country could not control alcohol during prohibition. There are similar reasons we cannot control marijuana. Both alcohol and marijuana are easy to make or grow and there is large profit in their sale.

Freddie and Fanny Provide the Explosives

For years, the investment public purchased certificates of deposit

(CDs) of Freddie Mac and Fannie Mae under the assumption that the full faith of the United States Government was behind these obligations. This misconception by the public gave a borrowing cost to these two entities only slightly higher than U.S. Treasuries. Most of these obligations were in the medium term and were shorter than the mortgages they were buying. This strategy increased earnings but increased their risk. Money raised in this manner, was the vehicle that was used to purchase subprime mortgages. In this way, the wishes of those pushing financing homes to those who couldn't pay for them were implemented. The executives profited immensely at Freddie Mac and Fannie Mae while doing what the Congress, court decisions, Acorn and numerous other agencies were forcing them or encouraging them to do.

These two companies were largely unsupervised by outside regulators. When members of the House and the Senate encouraged mortgages to those with low or bad credit, Fannie and Freddie took on this cause with breathtaking relish. This pumped up earnings in the short term. As a result, the executives got enormous bonuses. It appears this gusto spread through the industry. Evidently they and others did not set up corresponding reserves to cover the additional risks. They probably assumed that the housing prices would continue to increase and the borrower who was defaulting could sell the house to cover the obligation.

In addition to the accepted risks, they could not properly account for the transactions. Many in the business world warned of the extreme leverage (borrowing too much) of these institutions and the large accumulation of the mortgage market securities (Currently at 50% of the total market). Alan Greenspan, George Bush and John McCain were some of those who warned against the impending problems. Even the New York Times in their September 30, 1999 paper carried a column warning of the problems with the two companies. Whenever these critics raised these questions, Barney Frank and Chris Dodd were on television stating they were sound. John McCain sponsored a bill that would enforce some oversight and regulation on these two companies. Chris Dodd filibustered the bill in the Senate and Barney Frank evidently stopped it in the House. It's just possible that if McCain's bill had gone into effect when it was introduced, the enormous losses they incurred might have been avoided. At the very least they would have been reduced. The failure to do so is the result of the actions of Barney Frank, Chris Dodd and others in the Congress.

History is repeating itself. Many are encouraging lending practices with a tax credit as part of the package. A recent TV ad structured to look like a public announcement invites people to buy a home and finance it through FHA at 97.5% of the purchase price. Barney Frank wanted the agencies to reduce the requirement of developments total condos sold, from 60% to 50%, to qualify for financing. The reason it's important for a high percentage of the condos to be sold to qualify for financing as it can affect the condo's maintenance fees. If the developer runs into financial difficulty and can't pay the maintenance fees on the unsold units, the ones that are owner owned (the 60%) have to pay for the 40% of the non-sold units. That is a two-thirds increase in their condo maintenance fees.

The Speculative Housing Bubble

Without the underpinning of the results from the Community Development Act, the housing bubble may never have occurred. At the very least the speculation would have been less. The unnatural demand for housing came from two sources: the buyers who couldn't afford to pay for a home and the push to build so-called affordable housing in areas where real estate taxes were so high that buyers couldn't pay for the house and taxes. Builders became overly optimistic about the demand for the condos or townhouses. The design of these facilities was three to four stories and the necessary provision for stairs made them unappealing to most of the elderly, so they lost that part of the market.

There developed a feeling that a home was an investment rather than a place to raise the family. The real estate sales representatives exploited this. As a result people tended to overbuy on their home purchase. In the resort type areas, the speculators fueled the price appreciation with a process known as flipping, when the buyer commits to buy a condo or a home from the developer with the intent of selling the commitment at a higher price. This type of speculation drove up the prices of houses in the resort areas of the country. When the market collapsed these homes were dumped on the market.

This resulted in a glut in properties on the market where they could not be sold for the mortgage amount, many times referred to as underwater. A *Wall Street Journal* article of December 17, 2010 reported First American Corelogic estimates that 5.3 million U.S. households have mortgage balances 20% higher than their home value, and 2.2 million of those households are at least 50% underwater. The problem is concentrated in Arizona, California, Florida Michigan, and Nevada. This would suggest that the balance of the country is not in as dire a problem when speaking of single-family traditional homes. This also raises the question of equity, should states that fostered overbuilding be bailed out by the other states?

Reporting underwater home ownership on a macro basis is a disservice to the single family homeowners in more moderately troubled home areas of the country as it affects liquidity, price, and financing. It results in potential home buyers with a slanted view of how little they can purchase a home in an area that has few homes with mortgages worth more than the sale price. By reporting single-family homes, townhouses, condos, and HUD built affordable homes on a percentage of the market in each area give a more accurate assessment of the problem. It might mean that a resolution trust takes over the large concentration of defaulted properties.

It is unknown if there is a national inventory of residences by category, however it is reasonable to suspect that the large majority of properties in distress are condos and townhouses. Those mortgage-backed securities that cover only single-family homes in the non-speculative states would seem to be worth more. Wouldn't this suggest the speculative states might need to be handled in a liquidation manner?

The largest group that are the victims of these policies are the majority of the people who played by the rules of making sizable down payments, practicing restraint in their financial habits and meeting their obligations in a timely manner. They are the ones who won't be able to put their homes on the market and retire to a warmer climate or be able to sell their house and upgrade to a bigger house, as the size of their family grows larger. Congress focuses on the subprime properties but is less inclined to assist these deserving homeowners.

It is important that the single-family homes do not flood the market with foreclosed homes so at least this market will stabilize first. The layoffs in this recession have hit men with long-term stable jobs hard and this group is more traditionally head of married households.

In the past families bought homes because they wanted to live in them. Their expectations were a modest return and liquidity. They could trade up when their income and needs increased. The environment of the market blurred that concept.

Some of the people who couldn't afford to buy a house bought them, as they couldn't find available single and dual family rental homes. Traditionally, small entrepreneurs owned these rentals. They have been driven out of the business by unreasonable restrictions on eviction for nonpayment of rent, the restriction on eviction in winter and the avoidance of renters that do not treat the property with respect. They also feared the potential liability of sharing information on the history of renters. Compassion is in order but, where given, should be the obligation of the government and not a mandate to the landlord. The vast majority of renters are the ones hurt the worst. It's no wonder they bought houses they couldn't afford.

[TWO]

The Mortgage Crisis

The Attempted Cure of the Mortgage Markets and the Probable Risk of Future Financial Meltdown

There is a saying: "When you have dug yourself in a hole, quit digging." Evidently our administration doesn't believe that when it comes to the mortgage crisis. To this layperson it's easy to conclude that the actions of those in control of the mortgage markets and the financing of the outstanding and new mortgages are digging a deeper and deeper hole. Straws in the wind that point to this conclusion are:

On Christmas Eve the Treasury Department announced taking the $400 billion cap from what the Administration believes will be necessary to keep Fannie Mae and Freebie Mac solvent. (It was reported in an article of Peter J. Wallison in the *Wall Street Journal* Dec. 30, 2009)

Peter Eavis reported in the January 13, 2010 *Wall Street Journal*, The Federal Reserve had little or no mortgage-backed securities on January 1, 2009 but owned $550 billion of these securities by the end of 2009.

The "Review and Outlook" portion of the *Wall Street Journal* of August 11, 2009 reported that the Ginnie Mae or the Government National Mortgage Association value of subprime mortgage securities guaranteed will soon reach a trillion dollars. In 2006 Ginnie Mae guaranteed $410 billion, which is estimated to be $1 trillion in 2010. The *Wall Street Journal* of September 29, 2009 report that the Federal Housing Administration borrowing ratio (the leverage ratio) has increased as follows:

2006	14-1
2007	15-1
2008	33-1
2009	50-1

(Source: Department of Housing and Urban Development, Bloomberg)

Bear Stearns in 2008 had a leverage ratio of 33-1, which was a firm that failed.

The two housing agencies continue with high levels of debt, lower quality mortgages and contingent liability through guarantees. In the October 16, 2009 *Wall Street Journal* Opinion Page, an article by Peter J. Wallison, a senior fellow of the American Enterprise Institutes, has found the following, "Almost two-thirds of the bad mortgages in our financial system were bought by the government or were required by regulations."

"The FHA will suffer default rates of more than 20% on the loans guaranteed in 2007 and 2008." " When housing was inflating during 2005 and 2006, the FHA's delinquency rate was between 20% and 30%."

Mortgage brokers have been accused of predatory lending to unsuspecting buyers when they could not have done so unless the government was buying these mortgages. In the same *Wall Street Journal* article by Peter J. Wallison, "The data shows that the principal buyers were insured banks, government sponsored enterprises (GSEs) such as Fannie Mae and Freddie Mac, and the FHA—all government agencies or private companies forced to comply with government mandates about mortgage lending." Mr. Wallison goes on to state, "the Community Reinvestment Act (CRA), which required insured banks to provide mortgage credit to home buyers who were at or below 80% of median income." Since the early 1990's the government has been increasing its efforts in the expansion of the number of people with low income to own their own house. A praiseworthy goal, however, the unintended consequences result in a reduction in prudent lending standards, which lead to the subprime impact on the financial system. Freddie and Fannie were subject to "affordable housing" regulations issued by HUD, which required them to buy mortgages made by homeowners below the median income. This quota began at 30% in the early 1990's and gradually increased to 52% by 2005 and was a large contributor to the housing bubble.

Where is the outrage and demand for hearings on these failed policies? Unfortunately, these same people are continuing to push the lenders into doing things that are not good business. Worse still, it doesn't appear that HUD has reversed these mandates on the failed policy that has gotten the U.S. in trouble. Where are the hearings into the countrywide lending practices of "The friends of Anglos" and who benefited from this policy?

In summary:

- There was no guarantee of Freddie Mac and Fannie Mae two years ago. Christmas of this 2009 there is an unlimited guarantee.

- On January 1, 2009 the Federal Reserve owned little or no mortgage-backed securities and by the end of the year owned $550 billion.

- The FHA outstanding guarantees went from $410 billion at the end of 2006 to a projected $1 trillion in 2010.

- In James R. Hagerty's *Wall Street Journal* article of May 18, 2010 quoted the Treasury that one in four homeowners who were offered the governments modification program had been weeded out because they didn't make payments. The chart in that article showed of the 1.7 million who qualified there were only 295,348 that were active permanent modifications. Tales of exhausted savings were reported.

- To suggest that Congress can fix the problem it has created requires a suspension of disbelief. Barney Frank said they should get the profits from the TARP funds as well as those funds not used. It is hoped that this is not permitted.

How the Financial Firms were Exposed to the Subprime Mortgage Securities and How a Panic Meltdown was Avoided

In the fall of 2008, the banks across the world had locked up and money was not moving between the financial institutions to provide the financial liquidity to conduct commerce. In other words, financial panic existed.

A great deal of credit should be given to Hank Paulson (the U. S. Treasury Secretary), Ben Bernanke (chairman of the Federal Reserve), and Tim Geithner (chairman of the Federal Reserve Bank of New York), who helped implement his program. First, his recommendation for decisive action to the President on the TARP Fund resulted in President George Bush backing the plan. He went to Congress which quickly approved the fund. The aggressive implementation unlocked the banks and avoided a financial pandemic. Questions about the size of the fund, the requirement of banks to take money they didn't want and didn't need have not been answered. It's only conjecture, but logic would say the size was to convince the financial world that our country was serious about backing these major banks and the requirement that all banks take the money was to prevent a run on the banks that took the money. It would have been a statement that those who took the money were in trouble and the others were OK.

It's not clear if Bernanke and Geitner helped Paulson, who was the Secretary of the Treasury and the reports only talk about him strong-arming the bankers to comply. It would seem neither Geitner nor Bernanke had the authority to do so. In the final analysis, it was the President's, in other words, President Bush's program, as he recommended it to Congress, but he wouldn't be the only one who developed it. Doesn't it imply that it is Paulson's in the way it is written.

The original plan was to buy up the toxic assets from the banks. A guess is the enormity of the amount outstanding made this impractical so instead they funded the banks. This action was done in a matter of days. To their credit, they quit spending the fund at some $250 billion, as they avoided the meltdown. The balance should be returned to the people. The banks are paying some loans back; this money should also be returned to the people. After all, when they created the fund, Congress promised that all money not needed by the banks would be subsequently returned to the U. S. Treasury.

Some of the Johnny come lately have been criticizing, what they called a bail out. The President and Hank Paulson should be thanked for instituting the program and Ben Bernanke and Tim Geitner for their help, as well. Historically, they probably will be given this credit. Think of what could have happened if President Bush or Hank Paulson were a more deliberate decision maker and delayed needed action as they studied the problem over time?

The only non-bank usage of the funds was a swing loan to General Motors and Chrysler. This may have been different than their instincts, but the Congress held hearings and adjourned and went home for Christmas. It was close to the inauguration of the new president and this loan provided him with the opportunity to put in place his solutions to the car companies' problems. Can you imagine the outcry that would have occurred if the loan had not been made and General Motors and Chrysler had filed for bankruptcy just days before the new president took office?

The financial firms' problems were caused by the purchase of subprime mortgages. Some of the firms were ordered by the courts to reduce business credit standards to low income borrowers. The Community Reinvestment Act (CRA) required the banks to provide mortgage credit to home buyers who were at or below 80% of the median income. Those pushing their participation also regulate these same banks. It's easy to see how the officials may have been intimidated into aggressively pushing the program that resulted in subprime mortgages. There are those trying to absolve the government for the subprime mess while directing the blame to the private sector. It is a law that Congress enacted that was subsequently changed to lower the standards of the borrower. There were primarily two entities (Freddie Mac and Fannie Mae) created by Congress that provided the guarantees or the money that allowed the financing of homes that the owners couldn't pay for.

Added to this was the enthusiasm the banks and mortgage brokers took on this assignment. The added incentive was they could make a lot of money on these mortgages by bundling them together and selling them as mortgage back securities.

Corners were cut by the mortgages through non-verification of income, valuations of the homes that the mortgages secured and other means of verifying if one could reasonably expect the mortgages to be repaid. The rating agencies must have believed that normal due diligence had been made on each individual mortgage and the mortgage-backed security was what it was purported to be. They also must have been influenced by the valuations of the underlying homes, without recognizing these values were an inflated bubble. This resulted in approving a good credit rating, which made the security easy to sell.

All of the foregoing is what caused the problems with the banks. Concurrent with the banks exposing themselves to the mortgage-backed securities, they became proponents of high leverage (i.e. high borrowing). Had this not been so, they probably could have survived without the intervention of the government.

If ever there was a need for an outside non-political group of investigators to review the responsibilities of our elected officials, it is on how they were involved in the housing collapse. In every case the current majority party in both the House and the Senate has killed any such effort. It's sad but they continue to encourage these same abuses by Freddie Mac and Fannie Mae.

The business schools fell in love with leverage as a way of enhancing earnings. Many in the business world adopted this point of view. The members of management did not have the point of view of their predecessors who had been close enough to the experience of the depression to be more cautious.

The growth of retirement funds added to the 401K put enormous sums in the hands of professionally managed investors. Their focus was on short-term earnings and management's ability to hit consistently improved quarterly earnings. The takeover groups were predators that drove the stock down, in some cases with planted stories. They executed naked short sales (selling stock you neither owned nor borrowed) in a further effort to ruin the market on a particular company's stock so that they could buy the company at distressed values.

These pressures encouraged the company's management to try to achieve always-increased quarterly earnings. The practice of buying its own stock became popular, many times at high multiples, almost always over book value (tangible value) and many times with borrowed money. The effect of this practice would be to increase earnings per share while reducing book value and increase leverage, i.e. borrowings.

In the acquisition of other companies they generally purchased them for over book value (which produced an intangible asset called "goodwill" and did it with some portion of borrowed funds. In other cases it was a large portion or all of borrowed funds.

AIG got caught up in the housing market as they insured the financial document that used the mortgages as security. This is called a credit default swap. It is easy to conclude that they relied on the assumption that the underlying mortgage originator had traditional standards of scrutiny. They probably also assumed the party they were insuring had done reasonable due diligence. They were, after all, some of the largest and most respected financial institutions in the world. If this were the basis of their insurance, it would seem that both assumptions were wrong.

Attorney General Elliot Spitzer threatened to indict AIG if the board did not fire Hank Greenberg (*Wall Street Journal*, December 2009 Opinion page "Saying No to Spitzer"). He was the one credited with building the company. He was forced to step down in March of 2005. It is just possible that if he had remained as head of the company much of the ensuing problems may have been avoided, resulting in reduced taxpayer exposure. In an interview article by Holman W. Jenkins Jr. in the *Wall Street Journal* January 9-10, 2010, edition, Mr. Greenberg opined that, "the Wall Street firm Goldman Sachs should return some of the money they received at 100% on the dollar." The entire article is worth review as he said among other things, "previously these insurance contracts were paid off at maturity." Now he said these insurance contracts, require cash payments to be forthcoming to cover any drop in value or credit downgrade even before losses were realized. He didn't know who was the force behind the ISDA (International Swaps and Derivatives Association) change but said it is something that should be dug out. The amount of bailout money the taxpayer had to come up with would likely been less without this change. Why the government shows so little interest in his allegation is a mystery.

[THREE]

The Mega Banks: Too Big to Fail

The Creation of the Mega Banks

During the Clinton administration the Glass-Steagall Act was rescinded. This allowed banks to get into the investment bank business, which previously was not permitted. This set off a rush for banks to become the supermarket of financial services. The result was a wave of takeovers and mergers, creating the mega banks. In many merger cases, payment in cash was from borrowed resources. With the completion of the merger, the sum of the two resulted in less borrowing base for the surviving bank. Their effect was "too big to fail."

During this same period, many investment banks changed from partnerships to public companies. These firms seem to have lost the discipline of safety, which they had when investing their own money. With their new size, they could handle huge transactions alone. In the past, this was done with a group of investment banks. The former method not only spread the risks but it resulted in the wisdom of the combination of investment bankers. In many cases their compensation was in a division of the profits. In some cases, part of the bonuses to the partners remained in the firm as additional capital. After they became a public company they appeared to have the same mind set about their pay. This attitude may be the reasons for the huge bonuses.

A case can be made that the skills of the head of an investment bank are different than the skills required for that of a commercial bank. In almost every case, the experience of the CEO of the combined bank was in investment banking in others it was commercial banking. In banks that merged the two (like Bank of America), one important part of the business the CEO lacks is direct experience.

The risks taken in the derivative market are at cross-purposes with the traditional banking whose primary responsibility is to protect the depositor's money. Trading in the derivative market must be highly profitable. However, great decision-making freedom is evidently needed for the traders to function. These traders are by no means high-level executives with long experience in the field. There have been two merchant banks of long experience that have gotten trapped in trading losses. One was Barring Brothers where a rogue trader in Hong Kong, trading in the Japanese yen, forced this company into liquidation. The French Bank, called Society General, realized losses of more than $7 billion as they unwound their positions in the securities purchased by their trader.

Derivative market making should not be permitted as part of any American bank and for this reason alone commercial banking and investment banking should be separated; otherwise the depositors are at risk. When failure occurs, FDIC insurance must cover any loss. When considering risks to the taxpayer, what is the logic in permitting investment banks to have access to borrowing from the Federal Reserve by becoming a Bank Holding Company? A number of the investment banks made such a change after the financial meltdown occurred. Some of the other financial products also are high-risk activities. The auction rate securities are another example of these exotic financial products that produce high short-term profits but were risky activities. Auction rate securities are generally longer-term obligations that are sold to investors who want higher short-term interest rates. The technique is for the investment banks to hold a monthly auction of these longer-term notes so that the investor can redeem their securities when they need money. It works fine as long as there is an auction market. When there is no market, which happened during the market turmoil, the investors who thought they had liquidity are stuck with the longer maturing obligation.

It's very difficult to fix the banking problem without addressing how they book the valuations of mortgages. It easy to see how they are reticent to book them below the logical value. There is a saying, "The perfect is the enemy of the good." In the current financial market, this results in the banks and the regulators looking for the perfect way to cover every possible downside risk. This can result in a paralysis of corrective action. With the government's approval and input, they should go back to determine what year in the past is the current valuation of real estate like. For instance the current valuations are like the year 2002. Then use the local government's assessed valuation on the property that the mortgage is on and book that as the value. This value would then be used when considering if the mortgage is underwater. This might mean that some will be booked in error, probably, but on an aggregate basis will probably be rather accurate. The banks auditors and regulatory officials should accept the valuation for book purposes.

Congress is now trying to pass legislation to limit the chance of future financial firms' collapse. The lawyers are hard at work with, it's been told, a 1700 page document. With amendments, it is sure to grow. It gives unprecedented bureaucratic control over shutting down banks and other draconian measures. Some of our elected representatives think it will enhance the opportunity for financial problems, as well give a favorable competitive advantage to the big banks.

No less of an authority than Paul Vocker, former Chairman of the Federal Reserve is reported to have said in Kate Kelly's *Wall Street Journal* article on January 15, 2010, "banks that blend high risk trading with traditional consumer lending face unmanageable conflict of interest and should be broken up."

In December 2009, Senators Maria Cantwell and John McCain introduced a bill aimed at separating commercial and investment banks, essentially reinstating the 1933 Glass-Steagall Act that President Clinton signed the law that rescinded it. For some 60 plus years this act guided our banking system without major problems. Why isn't our Congress considering this bill? Its enactment would reduce the size of a number of our largest banks. If they were still to large to fail the country could consider Mr. Volker's advice and split them up. In what way are the mega banks needed by our society that a combination of smaller banks cannot provide?

Nothing is being considered in the Congressional bill to address the problems in both Freddie and Fannie that participated in the past problems.

Ineffective Financing of Small Businesses

The latest lunacy is the destruction of financing by community banks for small business through the recently passed financial reform bill, then subsequently offering billions of dollars to the community banks to finance small businesses. They obviously don't recognize that these banks will only offer loans that comply with the new law. There is speculation that it will take a year or more to write the regulations. Yet our political class wonders why banks are not supporting lending to small businesses. When they do, it will be on some ratio analysis that would eliminate financing of companies developing a product in their garage, like Medtronics. A similarly held view is expressed in Sara Wallace's July 2009 article in the *Wall Street Journal* titled "The End of Community Banking."

Most people think of small business as mom and pop operations and although these provide a living for those involved, they are not the driving force of job growth that the larger small businesses are. For purposes of identifying financing needs, we are using the term "small businesses" as having 1,000 or fewer employees. These businesses are not the ones that will be serviced by the national banks, many of which are mega banks. In some cases, such as factoring receivables, their primary resource for financing is provided by specialized finance companies, such as CIT.

With the bank consolidation, mergers and acquisitions into the mega banks these borrowing customers were swept up as customers. In most cases, the decision to continue financing, expanding financing or changing the terms are made at the corporate offices, many of which are in New York. This leads to reliance on computer-generated modeling of the credit worthiness of the customer. In this process, the line officers' personal knowledge of the business and local conditions that might affect the loan was either lost or was viewed as less important. As a result, these businesses lost increased financing that was needed, or their line of credit was reduced, or in some cases it was withdrawn.

If you accept the premise that huge companies will get needed financing no matter what the structure, no matter where the resource, they become the natural customer of the mega bank. However, these firms are not the source of large job creation. The small, emerging businesses can be the engine of job creation. Their needs are the support of bankers who know local conditions, have been a financing partner for many years and know the ability and integrity of the principals. This type of banker can lend safely where capital is less than optimal. The experience of the author has proven these types of medium-to-medium large firms have succeeded where better-capitalized firms with less character and skill do not.

The focus of the government should be to see that this type of banking channel is locally available so that these entrepreneurs can establish financing arrangements to fund their continued expansion. In the final analysis, this is the engine of economic growth that will provide the needed jobs for the nation.

As these firms get larger and larger, the local small investment bankers become the next step in providing their financial growth. They can help provide the need for public or private medium term debt financing. As the company continues to grow they need to help navigate through the requirements of an IPO (initial public offering of their stock). Thereafter, the small investment bankers become market maker and helps in shareholder communications. This results in expanding their shareholder base. In this way, it opens up public capital and financing, which provides the money needed to further expand the business.

The government's role in direct lending should not be undertaken or expanded, as it will not solve the problem.

Questions are raised about small company financing with the issue can the United States get out of the economic doldrums without a functioning and dynamic growth of small businesses with potential? It's the author's view we cannot with the restrictions placed on the sources needed by these companies and current environment available. The author was privileged and lucky to be part of the Toro Company, which made this journey.

To get from such modest beginnings, the company was changed from local over the counter, to national over the counter, to a New York Stock listed stock on September 6, 1978. To accomplish this, significant growth was achieved with good financial results and structure to an expanded shareholder base throughout the world. It took eight years to achieve this result.

Financing for the company started as short-term bank debt, with clean-up requirements, to a mixture of bank debt and medium term insurance company debt and finally achieving an A-rated public debt offering. Through all the preceding times, the company maintained an A-rated debt structure. This took about twenty years to accomplish.

Product was marketed through distributors, and the financial guidance of what was essentially a sales force was one of the facets of our obligation. Their retention of earnings needed to finance their growth was a key to our ability to grow.

In the early parts of the years after World War II, U.S. companies, including the Toro Company, looked at the export market as extra volume to the domestic business. It was a privilege to be a part of the international market as it transitioned to a business overseas. The challenge to this expansion was to find or develop importers that also marketed the product, dealt with multiple currencies, as well as dealing with different countries restrictions on our imported products. It was this experience that we learned how the U.S. tax code, which relies on a graduated income tax on our companies, reduces ability to compete. Most European companies are not similarly burdened as they are taxed in a manner that the tax is taken off at their border when exported.

In a year in which the volume of business was cut from roughly $400 million to $200 million in revenues, the team was required to downsize the company while maintaining its source of financing. It became apparent the difference between the New York banks that rely on the financial analysis declined to participate in financing. The regional banks that relied on not only the financial numbers but also the experienced base of the management supported us. We proposed a joint finance plan for a two-year period to give time to execute our recovery plan that the banks approved.

Layoffs were required which was done on a respectful basis where most of the employees got better jobs. Inventory liquidation helped our liquidity. Additionally, a public offering of stock brought us back to an A-rated, financed company. All of this occurred when Paul Vocker drove rates up to 20%. Those who left during this period could cash out at 100% of value as the fixed income portion of the profit sharing was in an insurance contract that allowed terminated employees to be paid face value instead of market value on their holdings.

One could imagine that our northern distributors were similarly stressed during this period. Through a number of actions we did not lose a single distributor to insolvency.

One further step was taken at a subsequent time. We wanted to set up an Employee Stock Ownership (in other words, an ESOP). The principal founder and CEO of the takeover of the company after World War II agreed to sell the stock to the ESOP. His reason, "I always wanted the employees to own my stock."

[FOUR]

The Global Warming Religion

The Non-Debate of Adherents of Global Warming

Those who adhere to the belief of global warming in almost every instance will not even debate the issue. To implement their agenda would have a negative effect in the electricity we use, the jobs we work at, the cars we drive and the taxes our citizens are forced to pay. The following chapter examines how likely is it that our planet will get warmer as a result of man's activities.

In an effort to understand what the climate change scientists believe, consider a review of the book by Joseph Bast and James M. Taylor, Scientific Consensus on Global Warming of the Heartland Institute in Chicago, Illinois. The authors examined the results compiled by two German scientists Dennis Bray and Hans von Storch and their survey of 530 climate scientists in 1996 and 2003. Only the answers on the surveys questions, where the scientists strongly held these opinions, were used in this section. Environmental Scientists, by their own admission, have a bias toward global warming. Those without strongly held beliefs are much more likely to be influenced by their personally held beliefs. Large sums of money are available, in grants etc., for those involved in the global warming issues. Many believed that you're irrational if you question the lack of science in these beliefs. There has not been a subject that the propaganda has been less based on hard scientific evidence. This is particularly true starting with the primary grades.

The work of Joseph L. Bast and James M. Taylor review of the scientists' survey found:

- Most scientists agree global warming has pushed up temperatures one degree F. in the last 100 years.

- Most also agree there has been no global warming in the last 50 years.

- The earth has been cooling in the last ten years and none of the scientists' computer models predicted it.

- Some nearby planets have warmed where there is no carbon in the atmosphere.

- Only 24.4% strongly agree that the United Nations Intergovernmental Panel on Climate Change, i.e. IPCC is a reliable guide to scientific consensus. The IPCC is controversial because it circulates "summaries for policymakers" that are written and edited by government officials.

- Only 32.1% had confidence that we could predict climate on a time scale of ten years. Only 27.4% had confidence in predictions of 100 years.

- More scientists strongly disagree than strongly agree that climate change is mostly the result of anthropogenic (man-made) causes. Interestingly the man who started Earth Day predicted catastrophic temperature by the year 2000, which did not happen.

Recently we find through inter-scientist e-mail they have manipulated data that did not support global warming. Keith Johnson in a *Wall Street Journal* article, November 23, 2009 reports on some of these e-mails. Gautam Nalk joins Keith Johnson in a *Wall Street Journal* report on January 19, 2010, "Climate Change under Fire." They report that Dr. Hasnain now says his previous assertions in his 2007 article in New Science, The Rapid Melting of the Himalayan Glaciers, was based on speculations.

Our schools have embraced Al Gore's book, "An Inconvenient Truth" with relish. There have been cases reported of children coming home from school crying because the polar bears will die. In other schools if the parent didn't come with the child and watch the movie, the child's grade would suffer. This isn't limited to the primary grades as others report on similar experiences through all the grades including college. It is not science, even its supporters agree, it's only a majority opinion and even that is suspect.

Paul H. Rubin wrote a comparison of the environmental movement with religions that is interesting and worthy of sharing therefore paraphrased excerpts of his article follows:

- While people have worshiped many things: We may be the first to build shrines to garbage (recycle bins).

- Have a holy day-earth day.

- Have food taboos. Instead of eating fish on Friday, or avoiding eating pork; greens now eat organic food.

- Have self- sacrificing rituals such as recycling. Recycling paper to save trees, for example, makes no sense since the effect will be to reduce the number of trees planted.

- Belief systems are embraced with no logical basis. For example environmentalist almost universally believe in the dangers of global warming but also reject the best solution to the problem, which is nuclear power. These two beliefs co-exist based on faith and not reason.

- Paul Rubin is continually confronted with recycling bins with several different types of trash.

- Universities are centers of the environmental religion. The schools should teach only those aspects of environmentalism that pass rigorous scientific testing.

The Resulting Coming Crisis in the Electricity Shortage

Approximately 50% of our electricity is from coal-fired generating plants.[1] The current Federal Administration with many States Administrations is committed to replacing coal-fired generators with wind generators of electricity. The most common goal seems to be 20% of electricity needs and the way they intend to do so is to use some form of carbon tax. This will greatly increase the price of electricity but will likely put some of these utilities into bankruptcy with the loss of their production of electricity. This reduction will almost certainly lead to shortages before replacement generation of electricity comes online.

The reduction of availability of electricity becomes more critical when increased demand is added to our needs. For example 5% of our current usage is from computers that wasn't available 30 years ago.[1] The most logical source is the expansion of nuclear plants, which currently supplies approximately 20% of our electricity.[1] Senator Lamar Alexander is campaigning to commit the country to building 100 more nuclear power plants in the next 20 years. None of which has been built in the last 30+years.[1]

There doesn't appear to be any ground swell of support for his idea and even if there were - it takes 10 years to complete a nuclear plant from conception. Much of this delay is from regulatory agencies. The need for electricity may grow even more if current plants are decommissioned. Vermont refused to renew the license on a nuclear plant, which expires in 2011.[2] Presumably they expect to get their electricity from someone else's backyard and the government will be required to increase the power grid to accommodate them. Even if Senator Alexander's proposals were embraced, the start would be delayed by legal action from groups that are opposed to any nuclear plants; a shortage in supply results.

Wind is only 1.3% of our electricity and receives up to $30 billion of tax breaks or $18.82 per megawatt-hour, which is 25 times as much as the combined subsidies for all other forms of electricity production[1] To achieve 20% of our energy needs would require 186,000 tall turbines.[1] Additionally the American Bird Conservancy estimates the existing 25,000 turbines kill between 75,000 and 275,000 birds a year.[1] Think of the impact on our environment from the killing of birds and the urban sprawl.

Solar power produces an estimated 3.2 kilowatt-hours of electricity in 2009. Solar power accounts for less than 0.1% of total electricity production.[1]   A study by Berkeley National Laboratories estimates the cost per watt of solar power in 2008 was $5.40 and for commercial use $4.20. This was after multiple government subsidies. Without the subsidies, costs average $7.50 per watt. Estimates on the price range of solar power vary from 17 to 29 cents a kilowatt-hour. That's compared to 7 cents for coal or natural gas.[3]

There is nothing more fundamental to a civilized life style than electric power. Without it, we could not heat our homes, could not extend our day through the nighttime hours, could not refrigerate our food and perform many other activities that use electric power. Yet, we seem to have a cavalier attitude by our politicians as their legislative agenda is doing everything that will make electricity less plentiful and more expensive while demand increases.

Those providing electricity must recognize the coming shortage in electricity. Why else would IBM develop a smart meter which measures where you use electricity? The department of Energy is funding efforts to increase those in use from 10% of the homes to nearly a third by 2013. A creeping change will influence such things as what time millions of people cook dinner and what kind of appliances they buy. Smart meters know when you're cooking, cleaning, and how cool or warm you keep your house. This device could easily be adapted to restrict the use of electricity (such as power for air conditioning as it is now doing, for a lower rate, during peak loads).[4]

With a shortage of electricity, would rationing be far behind? They could include restricting air conditioning below a certain level or only be able to heat up to a certain level. Other restrictions could impact our freedoms. Saddam Hussein used the interruption of electricity as a penalty for those he needed to control.

Every country in the world is doing whatever they can to encourage the construction of nuclear power plants. Hydroelectric generating plants produce about 4% of electrical needs. Since 1999, 200 dams in the United States have been dismantled.[5] Think of the opposition if we tried to harness other waterways or the tides. Senator Feinstein opposes building wind and solar generating farms in the Mojave Desert. If not there, where? Senator Kennedy opposed wind farms off the coast of Hyannis Port even though they are out of the sight of land. These are just examples of the opposition to alternative or green energy. This opposition could slow up their development by bringing the matter to court. These sources should be developed but will not, even closely, take care of our electrical needs. It's a little like fiddling while Rome burned.

One wonders, who is directing our economy? Is it Green Peace, the Sierra Club or some other group or combinations of all?

On the February 22, 2010, *Wall Street Journal* reported on alternative energy. It is worthy of review by anyone who feels our electrical needs will be met by a combination of all of current alternative sources. Among other facts they reported, China and others are moving ahead of the new 3+ nuclear reactors. The NRC certification for new plants in the U. S. may not occur before early 2012. Therefore, none of these are expected until late in the decade.

The Future Role of Wind and Solar

Today, wind is about 2% of our usage and no thinking person can believe they will take care of our energy needs. Yet this is where our Congress and our president are planning on spending billions of dollars.

Is there any thought that maybe these farms could have unintended consequences? What is the effect on birds or creatures that pollinate our crops and all kinds of plants? We banned the production of DDT because of its affect on birds. In the May 23-24, 2009 *Wall Street Journal* opinion page, the lead article started with the following quote, "In 2006 after 25 years and 50,000,000 preventable deaths, the World Health Organization reversed course and endorsed widespread use of DDT to combat malaria." Which, they are now thinking of restricting again.

There have been a number of wind projects that have been constructed that gives us some insight into wind power. In the March 5, 2009 opinion article by Robert Bryce, he refers to the latest data from The U.S. Energy Information Administration that the total amount of energy hours used in the United States for the 12 months ending November 2008 was 4,118,198,000-megawatt hours.

Valero Energy Corp. reported that they installed 33 windmills at a cost of $115 million and that the energy saved would pay for the installation in 10 years (presumably this cost is netted out after a governmental tax credit or other governmental subsidy). They predict that these windmills will produce 50 megawatts of electricity per hour. Therefore, one windmill would cost $3.5 million and would produce

1.5 megawatts per hour. If you assume an increase of 1% of new energy will come from wind, in the next 5 years, it would require 411,819,800 megawatt hours. Using Valero's energy expected production, the numbers this would require 274,546,530 wind generators, which costs $3.5 million for each wind generator. Does any reasonable person believe this will happen? Even if it did, a 1% compound growth in electrical demand over 5 years would not cover the electricity that the wind provided.

When the shortage of electricity comes, and unless the roadblocks to nuclear and to coal are eliminated, a shortage will occur. This will cause interruption in electrical service in areas of the country. Should other areas have any obligation to supply their needs when they cut their power production without providing for a new source?

The outrage of the populace will be so large that these failed policies will be changed. Unfortunately it will take many years to correct them. The lead-time necessary to build these plants is large and will be a drag on our economy for years. However, not to worry as the Congress will drag out their show trials to find out who is responsible. They need only to look in a mirror.

The use of energy savings bulbs has been mandated by Congress by 2012. There has been no consideration given as to the effect on the environment. There is mercury in the bulbs. The EPA has issued instructions on how to clean up if one is broken. Glen Beck's program followed the instruction on clean up. It included wearing protective gear, using paper to pick up the shattered parts and bringing the paper and the light bulb to a disposal site. Both broken lights and burned out lights will go into the household trash and, thereafter into the ground water. Then we will find Congress blaming others as to why this wasn't thought of? This happened a few years ago with a gasoline additive that was mandated by Congress and ended up in the water supply.

[FIVE]

Government Mandates That Ruined the Automobile Business

A combination of union work practices, healthcare benefits, and retirement benefits, higher than automobile average wages and government mandates on fuel standards has destroyed the American manufacturing of automobiles, known as the Big Three. Their competitors come from overseas where the populace is generally smaller in nature and without the vast distances to be traveled as the countries are smaller geographically. Therefore, the cars are smaller and consequently lighter and achieve good gas mileage. As a result, they don't need to design vastly different cars for the United States market.

The general demand in the U.S. market is for larger cars that have lower mileage ability because they are heavier, more comfortable over long distances, and safer. Overseas competitors can import their cars to meet increased mileage requirements (generally referred to as CAFE standards) American car companies cannot. General Motors had a diesel car made overseas that gets 55 miles to the gallon and, yet, they weren't able to import it, which would help them meet CAFE standards.

Our governmental officials constantly criticize the automakers for not making the cars the public wants. What they are really saying is that they are not making the cars the government wants them to make. The hybrid cars are stacking up unsold on the dealers' lots. Their mileage results are only marginally higher than the same car using gasoline, i.e. the Toyota Prius. They are on average $10,000.00 more than the equivalent non-hybrid. They have a huge number of batteries that need to be replaced periodically and estimates are at a cost of $8,000. It can be argued that minivans, because they carry so many passengers, (mothers with her whole family) on a passenger mile traveled, are the most efficient vehicle. Currently there is no company making a profit off hybrid cars.

The focus in recent times has been on the development of an electric powered car. The batteries add weight and the best hope is a range of 100 miles before the need to recharge. The GMC Volt has gotten a lot of press as the all-electric car. It currently is expected to achieve a forty-mile range using electricity. It really is a hybrid as it uses a gas powered motor to generate electricity increasing the range to 300 miles. The price is estimated to be $40,000. If history is any judge, there will be a higher price, hardly a large market at that price.

A call was placed to AAA and the inquirer was given the average yearly use of a car. The source of their information was from the emission standards report and was 12,000 miles. The electric car would need regular recharging even if the 100 mile range were achieved. It's not clear if the drag of air conditioning or heaters is included in that goal of 100 miles or if the two would reduce the range of miles.

The Obama Administration recently forced the takeover of General Motors and to a lesser degree Chrysler. In both cases, the secured creditors did not receive compensation, for what their secured position would have dictated on any previous bankruptcies. The unions received compensation and work rules far in excess of any other unions in previous cases. The union and the government own virtually all of these automobile companies.

The administration announced a committee to oversee these two companies. Two of the committee members, were reported to not even own cars; others were said to not own American cars. How can they possibly be objective?

The administration has said they want the two companies to make small fuel-efficient cars, as well hybrid cars. Their stated objective was to phase out the pickup trucks and SUVs. The company makes money on both vehicles.

Let's assume they want to get out of the business at some future date. If they follow their stated goals, it seems likely they will continue to lose money. Assume their first step would be to raise borrowings. Who would lend them money even if it were secured, when you consider how past secured creditors were treated?

The company is not making products based on customer demand with profit as its motive but rather on what the government thinks they should make. The result of the foregoing, it's believed, will be failure and it will continue to be a drag on the United States until the populace says, "Enough. Get rid of the company." The way it's intended to be operated will likely make a company the size of General Motors unsalable and liquidation will be the only way to get out of the business.

The ones hurt the most by this direction will be the union members and the states and cities where they reside. If there had been a more equitable distribution of shares there would be a multitude of shareholders and some kind of public market would emerge. Under the current arrangements the fear is the stock will be lacking in liquidity. Under these circumstances, large quantities of stock would be difficult or impossible to be sold to generate cash. How then, will the unions meet their obligations to their healthcare participants and those who retire? There is little prospect to generate cash to the unions until profits support it and under the current guidance this seems suspect.

[SIX]

Middle-East Oil Cartels Exposure

The Effect of our Overseas Debt

Our energy needs for transportation and electricity to replace Middle East Oil is nuclear for electricity and natural gas for transportation. There is no concerted effort to have a Manhattan Project for either solution.

Solving the dependence on the cartels effects not only energy but also our finances. Changing our balance of payment from negative to positive is the only way to solve our exposure to foreign holdings of dollars. With such a negative balance of payment for energy it is impossible to do so.

The stated goal of the administration is to be energy independent in 10 years. How can this be given any credence? Senator Lamar Alexander's article in the *Wall Street Journal* on June 11, 2010 states "Wind Power is not a realistic substitute for Oil." All of the Green energy solutions solar, wind, thermo and hydro are suspect in any time frame much less ten years or the eight years since President Obama made this prediction.

There is a resistance expressed as, "not in my backyard," by a number of ardent supporters of alternative energy. Senators Kennedy and Feinstein have publicly opposed projects in their home locales. These sources should be pursued when they make economic sense. They are by no means the panacea for energy independence or even independence from Middle East oil under the current policies being pursued by the administration. All the potential energy sources have small organized groups that are going to take legal action that will slow up their implementation. Therefore the two most likely sources nuclear and gas, needs aggressive legal defenses to get them implemented on a fast track.

There is no question we should be independent of the Middle East cartels as it's in our economic interest to do so. This should also include Venezuela and other similar suppliers. However when the implied goal is to get off the use of petroleum, it's an unrealistic expectation. It would be based on the hope there will be some magic formula that will power our vehicles. That doesn't mean we should not consider the environment but it does mean we should keep it in perspective. As an example, we should not destroy a project to save the snail darter. We are currently providing money to protect the marsh mouse in our so-called stimulus bill.

One of the most blatant tunnel visions on the environment that was reported in the *Wall Street Journal,* September 2, 2009 article, was when the "Wildlife Service" imposed water restrictions on the San Joaquin Valley to protect the "delta smelt." Tens of billions of gallons of water were diverted from the farmers. Drought conditions resulted in the Valley and the jobless rate has hit 14.3%.

It is difficult to reduce our dependence on foreign oil without creating a new supply. Our actions expose the U.S. to further gasoline price spikes. Those who want to do nothing assume the oil cartels will not cut their production, to drive up prices. OPEC's action in 2009 does not support this assumption. They also assume that if you throw enough money at the desire to replace gasoline there will be a magic bullet that will emerge; they are fond of giving as an example the Manhattan Project that developed the atom bomb in World War II. The difference is that was physics and we had Einstein's formula which provided the road map of where we were going. We have no road map for the so-called magic bullet for a different source of energy to propel our vehicles.

Canada is our number one supplier of oil and is also our number one trading partner. Mexico is the second largest supplier of oil and is our second largest trading partner. A continuing healthy arrangement with these two neighbors must be our continuing priority. Therefore we should continue to import petroleum products at the continuing high levels or even at greater levels from our major suppliers.

At today's oil prices the available supplies of oil will be less as the world exploration for oil is decreasing. Today's project valuations would not achieve the threshold return on investment to drill in the very deep waters of the ocean. Additionally the administration is planning to eliminate the incentive tax breaks for oil exploration.

It was reported in the Wall Street article of August 8, 2009 that the U.S. Export-Import Bank has issued a preliminary commitment letter to Petrobras in the amount of $2 billion and has discussed increasing their commitment. These funds are to be used for off-shore drilling in Brazil's Tupi oil field. If the Obama Administration supports off-shore drilling in Brazil, why not support off-shore drilling in the United States?

Our current government does everything to damage our means of supplying energy. The latest example of which is the House bill imposing a carbon tax called "tax and trade." The Senate has not passed it, but it shows a similar mindset. The House bill includes the production of oil, gas and coal. It will drive up prices for gasoline and will drain money from other uses in the economy; it will hurt our standard of living and will be particularly hard on the working poor.

The Danger of our Continued Dependency on Middle Eastern Oil

The increase in American debt to unsustainable levels puts the United States at risk from other countries. Particularly dangerous are the dollar holdings of some of these countries, the largest of which is China and Japan. This is reflected in our balance of payment account, which documents the products and services bought from outside the United States as compared to those bought from the United States. This balance of payment has been negative for many years and a large part of it is because of the importation of oil. Without reversing our balance of payments account to a positive or neutral amount for oil, it is largely impossible to obtain a positive balance of payment worldwide. Without a positive balance of payment worldwide, we cannot repay foreign holders of dollars except with dollars. What foreign country who doesn't want our dollars is going to accept dollars as payment for their other dollars?

The resources of the radical groups of suppliers, the Middle East oil cartel and dictator dominated suppliers, including Russia, will become even more dominate as our oil supply decreases and is not replaced.

The United States is doomed to be dependent on these less-than-stable countries unless we develop our own supplies. To achieve this, domestic oil suppliers need to be encouraged, or at least, not stopped by red tape or by other means, to drill in promising off- shore areas. This should also include new areas like North Dakota, Pennsylvania for natural gas and in Anwar. Failing this, we are doomed to repeat the high gas prices in the summer of 2008. This will negatively affect an already fragile economy.

Without decreasing our need for imported oil, our balance of payment will suffer even further with its negative effect on our currency. The more our dollar declines, the more imported oil will rise from this one factor. This will also increase our debt with other countries putting a run on the dollar at increased risk.

A case can be made that reducing drilling in the United States does not reduce demand. This being true, countries outside the United States will increase their explorations and drilling for oil. It's inarguable that non-U.S. countries would be less sensitive to environmental issues than those drilling within the U. S. influence. Therefore, drilling in the U.S. when you look at the global impact is more environmentally friendly than the alternative of the cartel and dictator dominated suppliers.

Add to this our dependency will increase because of our shut down of the Gulf Of Mexico drilling through a six month moratorium on all drilling, even those rigs that were approved. The moratorium will drive the big drilling rigs to other waters and according to people in the industry it will be years before these big rigs return or they may never return.

It would be naïve to think the other oil companies are not watching the way the oil spill is being handled by our government in its role in containment efforts. To what purpose is the rhetoric coming out of Washington? How is it in our interest to drive down the stock price from constant threats? It hurts retirees in both the U.S. and Britain, and the low price on the stock may well attract a suitor who wants to take over the company. What if it's China? Then explain how the Administration's actions were in the interest of the people in the gulf coast and the American people.

Ways to Reduce our Exposure to Middle East Oil

An announcement of the beginning of a coordinated program with strong public support would trigger a much more conciliatory attitude by the producing nations. The following it is believed would receive that kind of reaction.

The northeastern part of our country uses fuel oil or bottled gas to heat their homes. England once heated their homes with coal and with a concerted effort they switched to natural gas and got rid of the smog problems. A similar push from oil to natural gas would need infrastructure improvement in the northeast area or any other oil-reliant areas. The gas-fired furnaces today are highly efficient and are cleaner burning than oil. The conversion would create a number of jobs and thereafter as many maintenance jobs than before.

The use of natural gas are many and varied to convert our transportation to natural gas would require a stepped approach. The first phase would be to convert gasoline driven trucks, buses and other similar vehicles to natural gas. To support their refueling needs would require fueling stations at truck stops around the country. Research should also proceed on how to economically convert diesel vehicles of all sorts to natural gas. If the technology is readily available at a reasonable cost, encourage these conversions as well.

Offer a new line of trucks, SUVs and pickup trucks that use liquefied natural gas. All of these vehicles that were changed or bought new are cleaner-burning, lower in price and can be supplied from domestic production. There is plenty of natural gas in the United States that is from producing wells. There are also many very promising reserves. This substitute production would quickly lower demand from overseas sources. It would have the added benefit of reducing the oil shipped to this country in tankers. A program to convert cars to natural gas and manufacture a line of new cars would offer quick tangible results from imported oil.

Despite the accident with the BP drilling rig, we should drill here and drill now in promising off-shore areas, as well as areas of potential in the U.S. and Canada for oil and natural gas. Mexico could be included if the same level of common interest can be found as we have in Canada. Action is immediately needed to lift the moratorium on the drilling in the Gulf of Mexico. If this is not lifted immediately our dependence on Middle East oil will increase. Tragic as this accident is, the continued high level of pressure which forced oil out of the leak must be the result of an enormous pool of oil. This pool might be large enough to change the power of oil from the Middle East to the Gulf of Mexico.

Nothing in the above suggests that research should take a back seat to oil exploration but it does argue for fixing the dependence on foreign oil now and not wait for some hoped for solution in the future. Large expenditures for so-called clean coal should be made. The oil companies continue to spend large sums to develop other sources of energy. Exxon's work in developing natural gas from oil shale appears to be very promising. Their commitment to spend large sums trying convert algae into fuel is another avenue of research.

A push to construct nuclear power plants would reduce our use of natural gas. It's vital to our national interests to expand, in a dramatic way the increased construction of our nuclear plants to cover our ever-expanding growth and uses of electrical power. Failing this, will put at risk other avenues of initiatives.

A program to convert our freight rail system into a high-speed rail system to regional distribution centers would produce significant benefits to the country. The focus should be exclusively for freight. If in some cases the high-speed rails could also be used for passenger service, that would be an additional benefit but should not be considered when routing of the rails is involved.

Just in time manufacturing is a necessary requirement to stay competitive and is currently supported by a fleet of independent truckers. Sending these materials for the long distance part of the journey by rail, while focusing the regional distribution of containers by truck, could match and may even improve arrival time. This should result in significant cost advantage over current shipping arrangements.

An additional advantage to the country is that it would dramatically reduce traffic on our freeway system. This would reduce the need of forever expanding freeway lanes and would probably reduce maintenance of these roads. Where appropriate, high-speed rail service between cities would reduce the need for airport expansion. Examples of cities made for such an arrangement, are Minneapolis–St. Paul and Chicago. There also would be savings in the amount of fuel expended and the carbon put in the atmosphere.

The foregoing would quickly put us on the path of energy independence and dramatically alter, in a positive way, our relationship with producing outside nations, many of which do not have our best interest at heart.

[SEVEN]

The Case Against Abusive Lawsuits

The serious impact of the trial lawyers, with some of their practice like shopping for friendly judicial courts for their suits, cannot be over emphasized. It's one of the causes of our reduced ability to compete in the global market and for the escalating prices in the practice of medicine and prescription drugs. The Democrat Party, with the help of a few Republicans, has done much to insure that the some trial lawyers can continue to sue American industries, the medical profession and the pharmaceutical industry. There is plenty of criticism about the compensation of business and financial executives. It's hard to find an adverse comment about abusive lawsuits or the amount of money the trial lawyers make. There are an unbalanced number of lawyers in Congress, which creates a natural bias. In addition, the trial lawyers and their association generously donate to the reelection of these friendly legislatures.

Bill Lerach, reputed to be the undisputed king of class action suits currently sits in jail or has recently been release for the laws he was convicted of breaking (*Wall Street Journal* article by James Freeman, "Justice and Jailed Tort King"). There are some who specialize in malpractice suits, who regularly use a doctor that gives plaintiff-friendly testimony against the doctors and drug companies.

Some suits are initiated in Central and South American countries where they are filed against the American international companies in local courts. The *Wall Street Journal* reported that Superior Court Judge Victoria Chaney recently dismissed a suit of this kind with prejudice, which means they cannot bring this suit ever again. The judge cited a number of irregularities, heard evidence of U.S. attorneys colluding with judges, lab technicians and local officials committing subornation of perjury and doctor medical reports. Judge Chaney said the alleged behavior has "criminal overtones" (according to the *Wall Street Journal*, May 13, 2009, Review & Outlook "A Blatant Extortion"). It takes a suspension of disbelief that there are people who get lung cancer that smoked, but didn't know it caused the illness. There are cases where they file suits for damages even though the dangers of smoking have been known before most of them were born. For many years warning on the tobacco products are in large print on the packages of these products.

The legal community has increased the price of many items the populace buys. The ladder is an example. They have certainly increased the price of medicine from the malpractice insurance to the defensive medicine. Doctors are forced to do to protect themselves in case of a lawsuit. Many times the patient is told the risks of a procedure, and they accepted them and elected to go ahead. When the results were not what the patient hoped for, they sued the doctor.

Vaccines have a risk for adverse reactions, even death, on a small percentage of those who take them. However the risk of death is far greater to those that are exposed to the disease who remain unprotected. These deaths are particularly tragic in small children. Malpractice awards have driven most of the manufacturing of these life savings vaccines to other countries. As a result, can you imagine the deaths that would occur in the United States under a pandemic where there is only enough vaccines to inoculate the people from the country where they are made?

In a September 3, 2009 article in the *Wall Street Journal* they reported that a 2003 study from the U.S Department of Health and Human Services estimated that limits on malpractice awards would save between $70 billion to $126 billion a year. This doesn't include the cost of defensive medicine, which would increase costs greatly. Why isn't someone proposing reining in these costs in the current healthcare debate? The Workman's Compensation system might be the way to offer the victim recourse while keeping the settlements within reasonable limits.

The class action lawsuit, in many cases, is hugely rewarding to the attorneys involved. Those represented by the class action, many times, receive very little. It is not unusual for this group to receive notice of their inclusion in a lawsuit later notified it was settled. In some cases, those involved receive a small discount on their next purchase of the product or a small amount of cash. Companies cave in because it's too costly in time and money to fight the case.

The cases brought against those in the financial market by the investor that lost money is almost always due to the allegation that other people made them invest in the company.

The abuses of the litigant society are numerous but it's fundamentally driven by greed, with people and firms not taking responsibility for their own actions. How many times does the news service report that the ACLU threaten legal action against schools, cities etc., over a long time display of Christmas decorations or the Ten Commandments? These small entities do not have the resources to defend themselves for displaying Christmas nativity scenes and other traditional culture values. Therefore they settle out of court. Thereafter, the ACLU claims the suits were because of discrimination, as a result the government allows them to collect their legal fees and expenses. These abuses will continue unless we adopt the system used all over the world, which is the loser in a lawsuit pays for the legal expense of the winner.

[EIGHT]

The Two Legs of Debt Spiral: Stimulus, and Healthcare

The Effect of the Stimulus and the Healthcare Bill

The major initiatives of the Obama Administration and the Democratic majority are so costly that they put the government's finances at risk. Despite this, the Administration and its allies insist there's nothing to worry about. You don't need to be a financial expert to know this is dangerous. You just need to know arithmetic.

The so called stimulus bill that can better be defined as the long term special wish list of the Democrat congressional majority which, among other things, contained many, many earmarks. They claimed it was so important to immediately pass it, to keep unemployment below 8% that they couldn't even take time to read it. We all know its dismal results with unemployment at nearly 10% and higher when you count those who have given up looking for work. The excuse for the higher unemployment was "we didn't know the recession was this bad." Yet, before they took office, they were comparing it to the Great Depression. A case could be made that this was political posturing and may have made the downturn worse. Anyone who lived through the Great Depression knows the current downturn isn't as bad. It's just their handling of it.

The healthcare bill is supposed to offer more coverage to more people for fewer costs. The language in the original house bill says the following: if you lose your healthcare or change it you must go on the government-mandated program. There is to be a commission to review what treatment you may get. It isn't sold that way but it's exactly what the English and Canadian healthcare plans do. The president's intent is mirrored in his response to a woman's question, in a televised meeting, about her 100-year-old mother's need for a pacemaker, "perhaps a pain pill would be better." The Administration and the President admire the Canadian and English single payer system, but would not follow their way of handling malpractice. The House Committee voted down an amendment, which would restrict these suits. The high costs of medical treatment and drugs, plus the defensive medicine, are enhanced by these legal costs. If they were capped and restricted on a national basis, savings would be realized. The ones supporting the House bill plan to reduce Medicare's expenditures by $500 million. This reduction is not intended to make Medicare more solvent but to pay for an expanded entitlement. If history is any example, they would reduce Medicare expenditures either through restrict treatment or by restricting reimbursements to the doctors and hospitals. The result could very well reach a point where these medical providers could not afford to do them. This would result in their losing money on the cost of care or discontinuing their care of these senior citizens.

The bottom line is they are going to cut back the most on those of advanced age, the ones who built the United States in the period after World War II. There was an amendment voted down in the House Committee, which would have prohibited giving healthcare to illegal immigrants. Where's the gratitude for the contributions the seniors have made to the United States, particularly when these funds were going to cover people here illegally?

The healthcare bill that was passed was projected to costs less than $1 trillion. Since that time the budget office has issued revised projections that are much higher. Even these projections do not include the doctor fix for Medicare which costs millions.

[NINE]

Government Mismanagement

How Incremental Change Is Destroying Our Republic

The out of control heads of our different agencies calls for reining in their congressional delegated powers. The oil spill in the Gulf highlights the different agencies working at cross-purposes to the cleanup of the Gulf of Mexico. These past couple of months just shows how inept and languid handling of the cleanup is fraught with governmental mismanagement that does not result in being accountable for their errors.

In the *Wall Street Journal* (June 24, 2010), Neil King Jr. and Keith Johnson write that BP relied on faulty U.S. data when assessing the amount of needed containment. The U.S. Governments gave low odds of oil hitting the coastline for a larger spill than the current one. They assumed that most would evaporate or would be broken up by the waves. The government did not provide burning equipment when the oil was concentrated in those first early days. The reason was they had not purchased the equipment as a 1990s law required them to do. Additionally the EPA was and is, off and on about containing the spill by burning the oil. Additionally, in the first days of the oil spill our elected officials refused help to contain the oil from 13 countries (according to Speaker Gingridge on June 23, 2010). They continue to refuse the help. The Governor of Louisiana wanted to build barrier islands to keep the oil from the estuaries, weeks went by before he received permission and then for only a limited number. The Game and Fish Department closed down the construction of these barriers over their concern about how the sand removal would affect the fish. Another one of the Governor's solution was to bring in barges that were shut down by the Coast Guard because they couldn't find the life jackets. The barges were anchored.

The most outrageous example is HUD. To review: the 1993 GSE Act was the fuse and the trillion dollars in affordable housing mandates with the goal set at 30% of Fannie and Freddie loans. This goal was raised to 55% by 2007 (according to an article by Peter J. Wallison, senior fellow of the American Enterprise Institute, "Barney Frank, Predatory Lender" in the October 16, 2009, *Wall Street Journal*). Who authorized this? Was it some internal bureaucrat? Probably the single biggest contributor to our problems in the housing market and its attendant problems was this decision. Isn't it strange that nobody talks about it and there have been no congressional oversight meetings?

As reported earlier the Wildlife Services turning off the water to the San Joaquin Valley. These are not isolated or exclusive examples. During Katrina ice was sent to Maine instead of New Orleans. UPS or Fed X can tell you exactly where your package is, 24 hours a day. One of the most outrageous examples is the EPA declaring carbon dioxide a pollutant.

Representative Henry Waxman (Democrat from California) is one of the great practitioners of "get the bill approved then add to it later." On the Cap and Trade bill, he is reputed to have promised exemptions for the coal states: probably ethanol support for the farm states and other means of getting Senators from Montana, the farm states, West Virginia and other states to vote for this bill. Beware of these promised exemptions the mandate of the greens is to get us off of coal. Coal is the most BTU (energy) product in the world and the United States is the Saudi Arabia of coal.

Congress shouldn't delegate away its power to bureaucrats in the government. Where it has given away power, that power should be revoked. In other cases the function should be eliminated. Why do we need a HUD? We have a surplus of affordable housing. Some years ago there was a bill to limit the number of employees in the agricultural department to the number of farms. To their embarrassment they found there were more employees in the department than farms and the bill was withdrawn. Why is there a Department of Agriculture? Today's typical farmer has been educated at some of the finest universities on the running and management of their farms.

The Policy of Personal Destruction

Let's review some of the slash and burn of individuals, companies, and the vile treatment of those in authority in running these enterprises:

- Greedy Wall Street bankers.

- Mortgage brokers, who were given mandates to originate mortgages to people who couldn't afford them.

- Bank presidents who bought these mortgages.

- Rating agencies, which must have assumed the mortgage broke, used reasonable scrutiny as to the income of the purchaser, payment history and appraisals of the property. On this assumption, the rating was very likely approved.

- Car companies and the congressional committee's smug question about private jet travel when many of its members use government planes in a much more lavish fashion.

- Secured bondholders of Chrysler and General Motors as the Administration used a never intended legal maneuver to trample their rights. Many of these bondholders were in teacher and other pension funds.

There are also the workers of AIG who had legal performance bonuses on which many had achieved the requirements to be paid under these contracted agreements. The administration with their allies in the main stream media slash and burn these employees. These employees were further intimidated when forces of ACORN started picketing their homes. The result was they were not paid for money they had legally earned.

Early in 2009 the administration trashed the travel industry with the speech focus on not going to Las Vegas. This resulted in cancellation of group meetings going to multiple popular travel areas. The cascading effect was laid off low waged employees, loss revenues to the resort owners, loss taxes to the various government units.

Doctors have found their way on the enemies list. President Obama in one speech accused some surgeons had received referrals for unneeded surgery for tonsils and diabetic foot amputations. With this knowledge, he has the obligation to prosecute those involved so that the many fine surgeons are not tarnished by his comments.

The medical insurances companies, as well as the pharmaceutical companies are the latest to feel the wrath of the administration and their allies in the media. The medical insurance businesses are accused of denying too many medical procedures. There was a report that alleged that there are more turndowns in Medicare and Medicaid than in the privately operated companies.

The administration and their allies in the media quickly moved to trash those who are tired of the heavy burden of taxation and have protest assemblies with tea in remembrance of the Boston Tea Party. These were average citizens who were orderly in their protests. The only ones not orderly are those sent in to protest the protestor's. Look at the demographics of these supporters. There was a mixture of grandparents, ordinary working people and small business people.

How does one expect to receive support from those and others who might end up on an enemy list? These populaces slash and burn increases unemployment.

The double standard of our congressmen is so blatant they criticize the business executives in small jets while they use international size jets for excursions. The trips of Congressmen and their families are listed at $13 million. This is a jump of 50% since the Democrats took control of Congress. Alan Specter flew to Europe and the Middle East with his wife and aide. They listed the military jet cost at $571 a person. The true costs were in excess of $70,000. They did not list the cost of lodging and food and transportation of the two military officials was not disclosed. (The full report of these junkets was covered in the U.S. News portion of the *Wall Street Journal*, July 3, 4, and 5, 2009 edition)

The most recent outrage was speaker Pelosi leasing expanded luxury office facilities in San Francisco. Fox news reports that the lease costs $18,000.00 per month.

Trashing others to divert attention from Congress and the administrations may be good politics but it's terrible public policy, particularly in an economic downturn. What it does is create an atmosphere of playing it safe, which doesn't encourage risk takers to do what they do best, which is to grow the American economy.

The Policies of Increased Financial Risks to the United States

The United States and the rest of the world avoided a collapse of the financial structure by the quick action of Hank Paulson who convinced President Bush of the TARP remedy. President Bush then went to Congress for quick action on the TARP fund. With the help of Ben Bernanke and Tim Geithner, the collapse of banking subsided and they should all receive our thanks. The bailout use of these funds was distasteful to many, however. The quick action by Paulson and Bernanke, plus the follow up by Geithner after he was appointed Treasury Secretary should be applauded. The only amount used by the previous administration that was not intended was a swing loan to General Motors and to Chrysler in very late in 2009. This happened after Congress held hearings about their plight, adjourned and went home for Christmas without acting. Many believe the two companies should have gone into normal bankruptcy, probably including George Bush and his advisors, but he put his deference to the incoming President ahead of their instincts. The terms of the loan provided a short-term due date which allowed the new administration to pursue whatever course they wished.

There are a number of banks that are paying their TARP loans. These payments should be netted out against the original authorization and returned to the American people. The historical view of this action will probably be viewed positively. Dan Fitzpatrick's *Wall Street Journal* article of March 2, 2010 reported the TARP losses are now projected lower to $117 billion and not the $750 billion originally authorized.

The foregoing took care of the earlier problems however the unbridled spending, first with the stimulus bill, the healthcare bill and the push for the carbon tax bill, puts the economy at risk. As a result of these actions it also puts our currency and our country in danger of financial Armageddon.

One of the actions taken by the Federal Reserve is flooding the economy with money. Historically, this has made recessions less severe and of a lesser duration. One must wonder if this has been too expansive when compared to the past. The money supply is the largest increase in the past 50 years; it increased by a factor of ten, in other words approximately 100%, as compared to an increase of 10% in the past (Laffer Associates) Arthur B. Laffer's opinion article "Get Ready for Inflation and Higher Interest Rates" reviews the risks of this exposure.

Who really believes that with high continuing unemployment that the Federal Reserve will start increasing interest rates to curb inflationary pressure. The Chinese, who hold large amounts of American debt, have criticized the United States for spending their way into enormous debt. A little reported change is they are now investing in inflation-adjusted treasuries. What this means if their trillion dollars is converted to these types of securities, they will increase in value equal to the inflation. Let's assume inflation goes up 10% a year. That means their loan increases in value at $100 billion a year on a trillion dollars.

Tax receipts have fallen 18% over the previous year. Is it any wonder that people are less inclined to take risks to gain additional rewards when at every turn the government is hunting for new ways to punish through taxing those who are successful?

Mr. Martin Feinstein observed in his September 8, 2009 article in the *Wall Street Journal*, the deficit projected for the long term is a threat to our economic future. He outlined the March assessment of the budget deficit by the Congressional Budget Office, which projects a deficit in 2019 of 5.5% of GDP. It assumes that the economy will grow at 3% over the next decade and that the rising government debt will only increase the interest rate by less than 1%. The assumptions seem pretty optimistic and the deficit would significantly increase if just the interest rate assumption is higher. His article is compelling and would warrant a complete review of his thoughts, backed up, with in-depth research, from a man who was Chairman of the Council of Economic Advisors in the Reagan administration.

FHA is currently advertising for prospective mortgages from people under less than perfect credit requirements. This practice created our current problems. It is feared that high inflation, requiring higher interest rates will dampen or eliminate the prospects of a rapid and sustained recovery.

The burden put on our economy through the Cap and Trade bill, the expiration of the Bush tax cuts and the taxes imposed by the Healthcare Bill could very well create a financial tragedy with our currency debased and hyperinflation.

[TEN]

The Destruction of American Jobs

Environmental Destruction of Jobs, Coupled With the False Promise of Jobs

Prior to the election of 2008 of the Democratic majority, the mainstream media and the President denigrated the positive news of the economy. They emphasized every negative they could find or could misrepresent and then were surprised that people had negative feelings about the economy. Evidently their purpose was to win the election and felt it would all go away after they took office. Many in the administration are learned people, however their time in school must not have included how to motivate and inspire people.

In one of the President's speeches, he urged people to stay home and not go to Las Vegas. This is one of the most traveled destinations in the world. The Defense Department issued guidance that their conferences should avoid Las Vegas, Orlando and other similar popular spots. Many firms fearing ridicule canceled plans for conferences. The lower bookings put some of the casinos and recreational spots at risk. In an article by Tamara Audi on July 22, 2009, she referred to a statement by Geoff Freeman, senior vice president of public affairs for the U.S. Travel Association, "In the quest to demonize, travel we're killing jobs."

The attractive destinations became that way because there was a lot to do in the off convention periods. They also had the large capacity facilities, such as lodging and food at attractive prices. The jobs that were lost because the President didn't think the businesses should hold their conferences there were thought to be substantial.

In the hearings for the executives of the Big Three automobile companies they were denigrated for flying in private jets to these hearings. Compare that to the hypocrisy of Congress flying to the hot tourist spots around the world on military aircraft. These are not the trips that the military was going to make anyway. They are not on cargo planes G.I.s used, over the years, as a means to get home; they are luxury aircraft with accompanying military staff. Talk about a double standard.

When it became fashionable to criticize public company's private plane use, the car company executives and presumably others quit using their company's aircrafts. Some executives that were considering buying a new plane, we are told, canceled their orders. Cessna Aircraft, apparently because of reduced demand, closed its Oregon plant and combined their operation in Independence, Kansas. The jobs lost in Oregon are on the shoulders of the White House and those who made political hay out of the jet travel of the automobile executives. Where is their shame?

Money should be spent on the missile defense shield rather than cutting back on this program. These are very high paying jobs. We will need the most effective layers of defense against the expansion of atomic skills of unfriendly countries in the world. In addition, these countries have expanded their missile capabilities. Consequently we have a greater risk of a devastating attack. As a result, this becomes a must do.

The production of the new fighter jet will be stopped at 150 aircraft instead of its original goal that, if memory is correct, was 250. Presumably the military doesn't want additional planes. However, why stop the production? Some of our allies would like to buy this aircraft, Israel being one. However, Mark Helprin, in a February 22, 2010 *Wall Street Journal* article, makes a compelling argument that we should continue to make the original number of the F-22 Raptor as China will field their fifth generation fighter in 2018 or 2020. This would keep jobs, help our balance of payment, help an ally defend themselves and send a message to Iran on their behavior.

Which would the American people want to spend money on, the missile defense or that part of the Stimulus Bill for acorn, the protection of the two mouse species and planting trees in the Amazon?

The replacement of the incandescent light, with small florescent bulb will probably result in shipping jobs overseas. China will probably be the beneficiary of this requirement. China has a low cost labor force, and they are not burdened by the trial lawyers' lawsuits. The employees who get sick may or may not be caused by the mercury that they put into these bulbs but it will be claimed that it is the cause. It is difficult to believe that the American consumer will dispose of these bulbs in hazards waste depots. Therefore the mercury will find its way into the landfills and/or the water supply. Environmental lawsuits will result. U.S. corporations, including retailers may find it less risky to avoid making or selling that type of bulb. A review of the EPA's recommended handling of these bulbs if they are broken gives insight into how dangerous the government thinks they are. Besides the forgoing, they are not a good source of light. Proof of this is Germany, where this law is already in effect. There incandescent light bulbs have vanished and the costs of old fashion light bulbs have skyrocketed.

Congress has refused to put a cap on malpractice lawsuits, which should include the manufacturing and distribution of medical drugs. Amendments of tort reform to the Senate and House Healthcare Bill were defeated. If history is any judge, the lawyers' lawsuits will negatively affect the jobs in the industry. An example from the past was children's vaccines. The administration intends to save money by putting price controls on government paid drugs. Additionally, they are considering reducing the length that patents can run. The result will be less money for research on life-saving drugs, and it will put many of these scientists on the unemployment rolls. How do you get the companies to aggressively make swine flu vaccines where, doctors will tell you, in a small number of patients, some vaccines have a negative effect? Their view is the lives saved for the multitudes outweigh the risks.

The proposed Healthcare Bill will reduce others employed in the industry. The Senate bill has language that critics say will pay for some of the abortions. It seems inconceivable that the government will pay for abortions and not require all doctors to perform them. This being true doctors and nurses will leave the profession as a matter of conscience. Similarly Catholic Hospitals, as well as others, will close as a matter of faith, reducing employment. Both versions of the Health Bill requires one half a trillion dollars in savings from Medicaid and Medicare. The way the government has done this in the past is to reduce the payments to the doctors. Many doctors are refusing to take Medicaid patients or will not take on new patients as they are losing money on each. With the cuts that are proposed to Medicare probably will probably result in a similar fate. It isn't hard to predict that many doctors will retire earlier than planned. New doctors will not be attracted to the profession, as it is very expensive and requires a commitment of many years to become a doctor for limited financial rewards. Even if you are insensitive to the loss in jobs it will be counterproductive as there will not be the doctors and nurses to handle today's requirements much less the expanded requirements of those brought into the system.

One of the many promises of the supporters of the carbon tax is that it will create many new jobs and will make us energy independent; yet, they do not identify how much energy will come from each area and how many jobs will result. Let's examine if we could logically expect the results they claim will occur. Spain is the most aggressive country in utilizing renewable energy. They recently released their study that concluded that for every job created by the green energy it resulted in 2.2 jobs lost elsewhere in the economy (as reported in the *Wall Street Journal* (Europe), April 17, 2010 page 12). Valero Energy Corp. is constructing 33 windmills and hopes to generate 50 megawatts of electricity when the wind is blowing. To run these windmills they will need three employees. Each windmill will cost $3.5 million and each will generate 1.5 megawatts. T. Boone Pickens scuttled his plan for a giant wind farm. He ordered 687 turbines for $2 billion or $2.9 million apiece and expected 6 megawatts hours from each. Pickens would need 62 employees to produce his 4000 hourly megawatts of electricity. The cost benefits just do not justify the investment, the resulting electricity, or the job growth.

The job growth from solar is likely to be in China. The opposition to hydropower is probably too great to overcome. Thermal in areas of high heat generating activity appears risky. The potential job growth from clean energy will probably follow Spain's example one permanent job created which result in 2.2 other jobs lost.

Reduced Dependency on Middle Eastern Oil
Resulting in Increased Job Growth

The single biggest job creation for the United States would be to put through a constitutional amendment that would prevent collecting income taxes on businesses located in the United States. This amendment would provide a neutral revenue stream from a value added tax. Our competitive position in the World would immediately change, as this tax would go off for products and services exported from the United States. The additional exports would create new jobs and would slow jobs moving overseas and would likely encourage jobs to return to the United States. For it to work it needs to be a permanent move to a value added tax or the companies would end up with both income and value added tax and be less competitive. An additional benefit would be the collection of revenues from the cash society and a more dependable tax stream. An additional benefit would take money and lobbyist out of politics.

Open the national forests for road building and selective logging. None of the forests in Europe are treated in the way they are in the United States. The new roads would provide access to firefighters to reach areas that are difficult to reach. Cutting out dead timber will reduce the severity of the fire if it occurs. Selective logging will provide jobs for the small towns in and around our national forests and will allow the trees that are left to grow larger and healthier.

Convert the northeastern part of our country from home heating oil to natural gas except in the low population areas. Natural gas is plentiful in the United States. It's cleaner than oil, it's cheaper than oil, and there are many high efficiency furnaces that require only a plastic pipe as exhaust. The expansion of natural gas trunk lines would be required. Thereafter, house hook ups and furnace installations would provide several years surge in jobs. Service jobs would not be lost, as the needs would transfer from oil to gas.

A program that would start converting trucks and other transports of product, including buses, to liquefied natural gas would immediately create jobs. Additionally, the manufacture of a line of new vehicles would give a jump-start to the automobile companies. The profit stream from natural gas would result in an expansion of their product offering at the truck stops. When the public saw how the trucks cut their costs for fuel, it would drive demand for cars that use natural gas. At that time convenient stores would expand their product offering to include natural gas. This would probably require the service attendant of old who washes your window and fills the car with liquefied natural gas. The result would be employment for teenagers in a meaningful way. Can you think of the impact this would have on our importation of oil?

The expansion of a number of atomic electrical power plants would avoid a future shortage of electricity and would produce high quality, high paying jobs. Every country in the world has expanded its nuclear power plants (France has more than 80% of its electricity from this source) but the United States, who developed the process, lags way behind due to ridiculous red tape and regulations.

Drilling for more petroleum and natural gas in the United States, as well in the shallower off shore drilling sites would produce many high paying jobs. It would have the added benefit of buying less oil from the Middle East which would have a positive impact on our balance of payment and the resulting lower borrowing demands on the overseas countries. The current administration is lending Brazil $2 billion to drill off shore. If it's okay for Brazil, why isn't okay here? Of immediate importance is to lift the deep water-drilling moratorium. The commentaries on television say this has idled 15,000 workers with a monthly payroll of $330 million.

To make this conversion to high speed rail would create a number of new jobs. In some cases it would require a need to build new rail beds. In other cases it would require rebuilding rail beds. This could create many upper middle class jobs. It could also reduce the need for bigger freeway roads while reducing the fuel consumption of over the road truck fuel.

[ELEVEN]

The Danger of United States Financial Meltdown

Many economists believe that the high levels of spending, the increased national debt, and the acceptance of incredible amounts of contingent liabilities are dangerous to the financial health of the U.S. The worst-case scenario is hyperinflation, with skyrocketing interest, reduced economic activity, with the attendant loss of jobs. Other possibilities are debasing the dollar, with the loss of the dollar as a international currency. It also cannot be ruled out.

Steven Moore, a financial writer for the *Wall Street Journal* reported that the United States has borrowed more in the last six months of 2009 than in the last 30 years. Dick Morris recently observed that the Treasury is borrowing money at historic low rates and if it increases to 6%, a modest amount by historic measures, that it would take all the personal income taxes to pay just the interest on our debt.

There are several initiatives that are driving this level of excessive spending. It started with the so-called Stimulus Bill, added to this is the Healthcare Bill, followed by the Cap and Trade Bill, if it becomes law. We may argue about the needs and results of each. It would seem inarguable we cannot afford the risks of these massive spending initiatives. The question that has to be answered by the citizens of our country is this, are they going to permit those elected officials to ignore the wishes of the populace and pass these bills against our wishes? Communicate with your elected officials your wishes before they become law. When you consider the risks, remember a paraphrase of Ring Lardner's saying "the battle doesn't always go to the strong or the race to the swift, but that is the way to bet." Similarly, the economic results may not always go the way the economists, your common sense and economic logic would dictate but that's the way to bet.

[TWELVE]

The Myth of a Broken Healthcare System

When Congress shoved this Healthcare Bill down our throat they argued that our healthcare system is broken. Let's examine the basic premise.

Mark Constantia's article in the January 8, 2010 *Wall Street Journal*, referred to data assembled by Dr. Ronald Wenger. His revue was published in the Bulletin of the American College of Surgeons that highlights the excellence of the United States Healthcare. Some of his research revealed:

- Cardiac deaths in the U.S. have fallen by two-thirds in the last 50 years.

- Polio has been virtually eradicated.

- Childhood leukemia has a high cure rate.

- Eight of the ten medical advances in the past 20 years were developed or had roots in the U.S.

- The Nobel Prizes in medicine and physiology have been awarded to more Americans than to researchers in all other countries combined.

- Some of the most outstanding healthcare centers such as the Mayo Clinic, the Cleveland Clinic and many others were developed and are located in the United States.

- U.S. companies developed eight of the top-selling drugs in the world.

- The U.S. has some of the highest breast, colon and prostrate cancer survival rates in the world.

- Our country ranks first or second in the world in kidney transplants, liver transplants, heart transplants, coronary artery bypass, and percutaneous coronary intervention.

- We have the shortest waiting time for non-emergency surgery in the world.

- Even the WHO ranks the U.S. as number 1 of 192 countries for responsiveness "to the needs and choices of the individual patient.

We are in debt to Dr. Wenger for reminding us of just how outstanding our healthcare system is.

Millions of sick people from all over the world travel here and hope the skills of these outstanding doctors can help them. Sometimes it's to repair botched treatment in their country. Repeated surveys show that 85% of the people are satisfied with their healthcare and their health insurance, hardly a broken system.

Much of future innovation like the development and treatment for aids patients is likely to be hurt by the current healthcare bill.

The thing that is broken is the finances of Medicare, Medicaid, the Senior Prescription Drug Act and the program for children.

Aren't these the same Democrat Senators and Representatives who put these programs in place and in subsequent years their party line was, there is nothing wrong with the finances of these programs? They are also the ones that felt the Senior Drug Program was too conservative and did not spend enough money. It seems reasonable to suspect, that these same officials who politicized the debate in the past know that their hypocrisy would be apparent if they tried to individually fix the financing of the foregoing entitlements. The catch phrase they use is the system is broken.

These same elected officials have pushed through a huge takeover of one-sixth of the economy, in a healthcare bill that provides a $500 billion reduction in Medicare and Medicaid. Then they claim more people will be covered, at fewer costs and with better benefits. They must think the American people are stupid. Many of these same people admire the Canadian Healthcare System but don't want to rein in the abusive legal suits not permitted in Canada. Additionally the Canadian system puts everyone in the same category as far as waiting time and available procedures. In recent months it was reported the premier in Canada came to the United States to have heart surgery. He particularly singled out the waiting time and availability of the procedure was not available in Canada. Our elected officials, unlike those in Canada, keep their Cadillac plans and are not in the healthcare they provide for the rest of the populace. Late in June 2010 the papers were full of the financial problems of the Canadian Healthcare and how they will be reducing coverage.

The proponents of this change in the healthcare have another catch phrase "we can't allow people to be dying in the street." Dr. Constantian says our population has universal access because most physicians treat indigent patients without charge and accept Medicare and Medicaid payments that do not even cover overhead expenses. Additionally emergency hospital treatment must be given even if the patient cannot pay for it

The solution is to attack these program costs individually and don't mask it under a healthcare bill that will increase the likelihood of severe economic problems. The program that was passed "transfers funds from the old to the young" (according to Janet Adam in the *Wall Street Journal*, July 26, 2010), and it would also transfer money from the old to illegal aliens if those who want to give them amnesty get their wish.

[THIRTEEN]

The Road to Economic Ruin from Healthcare, Finance Reform and the Proposed Carbon Bill

The Cap and Trade bill probably is or near the top of the list of bad bills passed by the House of Representatives in recent years. This bill limits carbon emissions in a draconian manner for the United States.

These carbon emissions are tightened even further in subsequent years. If the requirement is not met, one can buy surplus carbons from others or shut down. Those who reduce carbons, like planting trees can sell the surplus carbons.

Even the proponents of this bill admit if the program were completely implemented in the United States it would not effect carbon emissions on a global scale. Russia, China, Brazil and India, are not going to reduce their carbon footprint but are, in fact, increasing it with, among other things, coal-fired electrical generators.

The trading of carbon emissions is a way of taxing currently untaxed activities, with the decision to do so by an unelected bureaucrat called the Environmental Protection Agency. If enacted, carbon credits would be one of the largest commodities to be traded. They will make Wall Street traders fabulously wealthy. One must ask how does buying carbon credits from one source and selling it to another change the world's carbon footprint?

China, Russia, Brazil and India understand what others in the Western World do not- that this will decrease economic activity, create larger unemployment, reduce the standard of living and increase poverty. Evidently our congress doesn't care if this bill's effect is to destroy jobs. Those who support the green movement argue it will create jobs, jobs and more jobs. As this seems to be the underpinning of why there is support for this bill, we must ask, "where will these jobs be?"

Wind generation probably has some limited application but nowhere enough to replace some portion of our existing electrical requirements. However, we must first know what impact this has on nature's ability to pollinate plants. There is early evidence that these wind generators kill birds. What is the effect of that on the environment? We banned DDT because it either killed birds or reduced birds being born at the cost of millions of lives, from malaria every year. Since the inception of the ban, the worldwide preventable deaths from malaria have been estimated to be 50,000,000, many of which were children.

An October 30, 2009 *Wall Street Journal* article reported that the evidence suggests the jobs are going overseas. Cappy McGarr, managing partner of the "U.S. Renewable Energy Group", was quoted they would seek tax credits and support from the stimulus package for its 600 million megawatt development.

McGarr said the project would create 2800 jobs with only 15% being in the United States. The Chinese are providing $1.5 billion in financing this project. He further reports that global manufacture of wind turbines after 1980 shifted to Europe. The manufacture of wind turbines, supported by Chinese financing power and lower labor costs, now appears is heading for China. The Chinese solar industry has expanded capacity and driven down prices and with these synergies, will be able to undercut American manufacture. Even if the solar and wind energy would create jobs, it seems likely they will be created overseas and the jobs lost for the energy they replace will either not create jobs or will lose jobs if it replaces current energy production.

Spain reported that for every job that was created, from green energy, 2.2 jobs were lost. It also was their experience that for every nine jobs created for green energy only one was permanent. It seems clear that the experience in Spain and the trends in China on trends on the manufacture of wind generator will cost jobs in the United States. The claimed creation of jobs and the green energy technology that is currently pointed to, as a solution, is suspect.

These risks to our economy are taken when the underlining push for green energy is coming from the United Nations' Intergovernmental

Panel on Climate Change. Their widely circulated "summaries for policymakers" are written and edited by governmental officials not by scientists. Of the climate scientists' opinions from which their policy was developed only 24.4% strongly agreed that the IPCC reports accurately reflected the consensus of thought within the scientific community (according to the Bast and Taylor review "Survey of Climate Scientists").

Recently, the peer reviewed journal, *Science*, led by Princeton's Tim Searchinger, pointed to "a critical accounting error" in the way biofuels are measured in programs of worldwide climate change. The Science study argues this is a false conclusion because it doesn't consider changes in land use. If mature forests were cleared for biofuel-growing farms then the carbon used by these forests would increase carbon. Ethanol actually generates the same amount of greenhouse gas as fossil fuel, in other words petroleum. Representative Henry Waxman's Energy and Commerce Committee cap and trade program banned the Environmental Protection Agency from studying land-use changes. This bill passed with the votes of farm state Democrats. (For a complete review of this article it can be found on the editorial page of the October 30, 2009 *Wall Street Journal*.)

A review of an article by Jeffrey Ball in the Oct. 30, 2009 *Wall Street Journal* shows how convoluted the climate scientists opinions are. It's hard to conclude we should take the drastic steps of cap and trade under these conditions.

[FOURTEEN]

Insights and Challenges

It's hard to recall that President Bush complained that he inherited President Clinton's recession. However, President Obama regularly complains that he inherited President Bush's recession. A comparison of the two may bring some insight into their respective challenges, their actions and the results that followed.

There was nothing that President Bush had any hand in that gave him responsibility for the collapse of the dot-com bubble and the recession that started in the early 2000's followed up with the destruction of the World Trade Center, on Sept 11, 2001. This resulted in further stress to the economy. The Bush administration recommended a large tax cut, combined with early passage, as a remedy for the failing economy.

There was a late 2007 recession caused by the housing bubble collapse. In September 2008 there was a worldwide banking crisis caused by a collapse of the housing bubble prices. Hank Paulson with President Bush's backing recommended to Congress a TARP bail out to some of the major banks. The program worked and the crisis was avoided. President Obama was not responsible for this collapse. However, the Democratic majority sowed the seeds of this problem.

President Carter enacted the Community Development Act which became the seed of selling houses to people that could not afford to pay for them. President Clinton signed the repeal of the Glass-Steagall Act, which permitted banks to own or become a part of an investment bank. Thereafter, many became involved in derivates and other high-risk investment banking activities.

It became obvious that Freddie Mac and Fannie Mae needed some government involvement, or oversight, as the public's perception was that the obligations were government guaranteed. Senator John McCain, with other sponsors prepared a bill in late 2005 that would have provided the government watchdogs. Chris Dodd filibustered the bill and it never came up for a vote. It had a similar fate in the House. Is it just possible that had that bill been enacted the housing bubble might have been avoided, or at the very least reduced the severity of the housing crisis.

A quick review on how the two were handled. The stock market meltdown was similar in nature.

Bush put in new tax cuts with much of going to the lower economic class. The Governments tax revenue increased. The unemployment top level was 8%. At the end of 18 months it was 6.5%

Obama put in an $800 billion stimulus bill. The government's tax revenue decreased. The top unemployment level was 10.5%. At the end of 18 months the unemployment level was 9.5%

Needed Changes in Wall Street

The Banks should not be permitted to be in the investment banking business. The reasoning for this is that never again should the public's deposits in the banks be at risk for investment banking activities. If this means the Glass-Steagall Act should be reintroduced then this should be authorized. Similarly, the investment banks should not have a call on the (The Window) Federal Reserve for borrowed funds. When two of the largest investment banks, changed to bank holding companies, it permitted them to borrow directly from the Federal Reserve. When the Federal Reserve lends to the investment banks, that money is at risk for same kind of activities that created the too big to fail problems. Additionally, the general public feels there is an implicit guarantee by the Federal Reserve as a result they can borrow at a lower rate than their financial structure would dictate. This is similar to how the public viewed lending to Freddie Mac and Fannie Mae, in the past.

Additionally where is the outrage where the banks and investment banks make enormous profits by borrowing at essentially zero interest and lending to the government at a higher rate. This is transferring earnings from the savers to the banks and investment banks. Logic would tell you that a large portion of this transfer of earnings is coming from the elderly. In the discussions in the past about the inheritance tax there have been reports about how much of this pool of cash is held by this group.

The Mega banks were created essentially through mergers. Those banks that have become too big to fail should reverse the mergers and sell off, these regional banks. The test should be is the deposits of the investors at risk without the government's intervention, if so, they should be required to reduce their requirements for capital through divestitures or raise capital.

The public needs to be assured that the companies are keeping the depositors interest in perspective. No reasonable person believes these enormous compensation packages are in order for the chief executives of these companies, including the large public financial institution. That does imply that the government should be involved in setting salaries, as they should not. If you look at how these salaries ballooned it started when Congress changed the tax laws. Thereafter executive salaries over a certain amount could not be deducted as an expense. This resulted in stock options as an additional source of income to the executives. The options were not expense items. They were dilative to shareholder earnings, which most investors ignore.

The solution to a more accountable management is to designate, by law, that the chairman of the board will be different than the CEO. The duties of the Chairman would be to only represent the shareholders' long-term interests. This would include keeping leverage under control and would limit the chase for short-term earnings at the expense of long-term earnings results. In addition the proxies should go to the chairman of the board with control over their votes. The human resource executive should report directly to the board on matters of the top executive's compensation. The chairman of the board, with the executive committee, would identify the type of experience background each board member should have. The human resource executive would also help create job descriptions for each of the board of directors. The job description would guide those being recruited. This type of a structure would keep these ridiculous compensation packages under control. It would also stop the politically correct board of directors and replace them with those who can help guide the company. This would truly have the CEO's reporting to the advocate for the shareholders, the chairman of the board and the directors.

The Loss of Swagger and the Need for a Confident Style

It is difficult to see how the current recession can end in any meaningful way without the return of swagger to our people, to our business community and government. Why, you may ask, is this important? They are the risk takers. Most important achievements are by risk takers.

Our current administration appears to be doing everything it can to create a swagger-less society. Many call it the Chicago style of politics. It may be good politics but it's a lousy economic stimulus. People with confident airs tackle seemingly impossible tasks with success. The current climate of foxhole mentality of our population and of our business leaders and with the herd mentality of many of our elected officials will bring our country on the cliff of disaster if it does not stop,

We must bring swagger back to our population. With all the criticism leveled at every level of our society it is an enormous task. Why not start with the old saying: "Be critical in private and praise in public", or "If you can't say anything good about someone say nothing."

This does not say you can't disagree with the policies of the government. Disagree with as much passion as you wish and without fear of ridicule or retribution, for that is the very essence of democracy. Jefferson once said if you are afraid of the government that's tyranny; if the government is afraid of the people, that is freedom. How would you rate the United States now?

The fork in the path of direction for the United States

In many ways the people of the United States are like Gulliver when he fell asleep in Lilliput and he woke and found himself tied to the ground by the Lilliputians. In our case it's not the Lilliputian's rope but the EPA, OSHA, Department of Energy, Water Management, Fish & Game Administration, Department of Education, Political Correctness, ACLU, and many other of the federal and state governments that have captured us and taken away our freedom. Nonelected, unconfirmed, tunneled vision zealots generally run these departments with accountability to no one. Many times they are at cross-purposes when a gulf-type accident happens.

How could you conclude otherwise? Let's use the example of the

Gulf oil spill. Time will probably tell if it is a freak of nature, an error in judgment or a risky procedure. After it happened it was the federal government's responsibility to see that the containment of the spill was done in as efficiently and as timely a manner as possible. Let's review the bidding as they say in bridge.

Big oil companies base their plans for responding to an oil spill larger than the current one on U.S. government projections that gave very low odds of it hitting shore. The government's 2004 model assumed most of the oil would evaporate or get broken up by big waves.[1] This probably explains the delayed response by the administration.

One of the first steps in containment is immediately set the oil on fire when the oil is concentrated near the spill. Congress passed a law several years ago that the government should buy a number of the rigs that is used to start the oil fires. The department in charge hadn't purchased the rigs. Additionally the EPA wasn't sure they could do this unless they studied the effect on air quality.

It has been reported that several European countries offered help with skimmers to contain the oil from the beaches. The Jones Act prevents foreign-crewed ships to do this. This act was waived, by the Bush administration for Katrina and was not waived by the Obama Administration and the help was turned down.

The Governor of Louisiana wanted to build artificial island barriers to stop the oil from getting into the estuaries. He received no response for weeks and when approved covered only a few of his request. Construction was started on these barriers and it was shut down by the Game and Fish Department, as they worried how digging up the sand would affect the fish.

The State of Louisiana moved in barges to protect the shore. The Coast Guard shut it down, it was reported, for lack of life vests and knowledge of ownership of the barges that were at anchor.

It was also reported that the beach workers were restricted in the amount of time worked by OSHA related to the heat. Did they take into account that tourists flock to the beach, at this time of year to enjoy the cool sea breezes coming off the water?

The Admiral of the Coast Guard has been given the responsibility to run the Gulf spill yet there are all these detractors who are going to interject delay as a best case and at worst case shut down needed cleanup.

The bureaucratic structure works at cross purposes with trying to improve the economy. An example is the moratorium on Gulf oil drilling. This just adds to the economic malady resulting in core unemployment at 9.5%. The real unemployment is much higher when those are added who have given up looking for work. Many in the current administration are confirming this with their belief that core unemployment will stay at or above current levels as a structural part of the economy. This was the stance taken by the Carter Administration before President Reagan changed the course of the government and the economy responded.

Think of the anchor this is to the business community, particularly the small businesses. This is the part of the economy for new job growth. This bureaucratic machine must be dismantled to invigorate the economic health of the United States. Some of the agencies must be permanently closed. That's a new idea, can you recall any that have been closed in the past. In other cases, Congress must rescind the delegated authorities and where needed for operational purposes replaced by iron clad guidelines of what the agencies cannot do. A yearly audit should be conducted by an outside group to see that the agency is complying with the law congress passed. It's only then we will get back many of our individual liberties that have been trampled on.

To repeat, Thomas Jefferson once said, "When you are afraid of your government, that is tyranny. When the government is afraid of you, that is freedom."

Additional Notes and References

From Edward Pinto, Chief Financial Officer Fannie Mae from 1967 to 1998, in a *Wall Street Journal* article, November 13, 2009, the following are portions or paraphrases: Everyone agrees that the bursting of the bubble caused the financial collapse in 2008. Most agree that the housing bubble started in 1997.

The Carter Administration's "Community Development Reinvestment Act" was a watershed moment. With the Clinton Administration's passage of the 1992 Federal housing Enterprises Financial Safety and Soundness Act known as the GSE Act, Acorn and other liberal groups got Congress to mandate innovating and flexible lending practices, such as higher debt ratios and creative definitions of income. It was the fuse that lit the trillion dollars of affordable housing loans and resulted in the housing bubble.

From 1977 to 1991 $9 billion in CRA loans were made, Congress signaled to GSEs they should accept loans with 5% or less, ignore impaired credit and otherwise loosen lending guidelines. Total loans rose to $6 trillion and down payments of 5% or less went from 9% in 1991 to 27% in 1995 to 29% in 2007.

Allen Fishbein at the Federal Reserve noted in a speech that ACORN and other community groups were informally deputized by the House Banking Chairman Henry Gonzalez to draft statutory language setting the law's affordable housing mandates.

Now history may repeat itself as many of these same community groups are pushing congress to expand these mandates to all mortgage lenders.

The Citizens Magazine of May 2009 describes how banks were forced to comply with mandates put in place by the Clinton Administration in September of 1994: implemented a new set of regulations that would score banks on their compliance. Experts lined up to warn Congress of the impending crisis:

Dr. Lawrence H. White described the impact of the new regulations: Regulators could now deny a bank with low CRA approval to merge with another bank at a time when the arrival of interstate banking made such approvals especially valuable. It even required approval to open a new branch.

There would be no "A for effort." Bank examiners would use Federal Home Loan data broken down by neighborhood; income group and race to rate bank's Left Wing groups were even given a voice in the ratings.

William A Niskanen, Chairman of the Cato group, warned that Clinton's new regulation would be costly to the economy, the banking system and to the communities.

Harvard's Professor Hal Scott told a Washington audience in 1995 Bank safety and soundness may be significantly eroded.

In 2000 Jeffery Gunther of the Federal Reserve Bank of Dallas documented a highly detailed analysis of CRA'S lending activities. His analysis showed that aggressive lending standards helped CRA but hurt safety and soundness ratings of banks

Former Senator Phil Gramm Sponsored a bill to fix CRA'S problems but Clinton threatened to veto the bill.

Gunther of the Federal Reserve predicted in 2000 "the conflict between the CRA and safety and soundness may not receive the remedial attention until the next round of asset quality problems. He in fact was predicting the sub-prime loan problems.

Economist Russell Roberts., of the George Mason University, describes how these goals increased. The original goal of the CRA legislation was for 30% of the loans originated by Fannie and Freddie would comply with CRA mandates. In 1996 HUD raised this to 42% then targeted increases to 50% in 2000 and 52% in 2005. Roberts reported that in 1996 HUD required that 12% of all mortgages purchased by Freddie and Fannie be with borrowers with incomes of less than 60% of median income. HUD raised this percentage to 20% in 2000, 22% ion 2005 and their goal was 28% in 2008

The New York Times reported in 1999 that Fannie Mae was under increased pressure from the Clinton administration to expand mortgages to low and moderate-income people. The road to melt down was firmly in place,

In March of 2008 memos to President Bush from treasury secretary Henry Paulson singled out the subprime mortgages as the single trigger to recent events. In other words, they triggered the collapse of the housing bubble.

The *Wall Street Journal* reported on April 10, 2010 that Alan Greenspan, former Chairman of the Federal Reserve, in testimony to the panel investigating the origin of the financial crisis, argued that any excessive move by the Federal Reserve to restrict sub-prime lending would be quashed by Congress. They saw such loans to individuals with poor credit as an important tool in boosting homeowners. He also argued that Fannie and Freddie piled into the subprime market to meet congressional pressure.

Peter J. Williams, a senior fellow from The American Economics Institute, made the following observations in the *Wall Street Journal* of October 16, 2009:

Almost two thirds of the bad mortgages in our financial system were bought by government agencies or were required by law. Since early 1990 the government has attempted to expand home ownership in full disregard of prudent lending principles. If the financial crisis's was caused by subprime mortgages it was the governments own policies that made it happen.

Stan Liebowitz is professor of economics and shared with the *Wall Street Journal* his "regressive analysis of loan level data on 30 million mortgages compiled by McDash Analysis." His conclusion: "zero down mortgages not subprime led to the mortgage meltdown." His analysis indicates that by far the most important factor related to foreclosures is the extent to which the homeowner has or ever had a positive equity in the home. If substantial down payments had been required the housing bubble would have been certainly smaller, if it incurred at all. Professor Liebowitz went on to say we are at a crossroads where we can undo the damage to the housing market by strengthening the underwriting standards in a reasonable way. But to do so political leaders must face up to the actual cause of the mortgage crisis not fictional causes that fit political agendas and election strategies.

David Luhnow in December 26-27, 2009 wrote "Saving Mexico," in which he quoted a Mexican Official who said "Economically there is no argument or solution other than the legalization of at least marijuana."

In February 21-22, 2010 David Luhnow and Jose DeCordoba quoted another Mexican official "The Mexican State is in danger. We are not yet a failed State. But if we don't take action soon we will become one very soon.

In the February 23, 2009 *Wall Street Journal* opinion page, Mr. Cardoso former President of Brazil; Cesar Gaviria, former President of Colombia; and Mr. Zedillo former President of Mexico concluded "The War on Drugs is a failure."

Stephanie Simons reported in the *Wall Street Journal* about the growth in pot plantations in our national forests.

Nick Wingfield in *U.S. News and World Report* relates that "The push for looser pot laws gains momentum."

An article by Mr. Banks, who covers the border for the *Tucson Weekly* reports on "Our lawless Mexican Border" He reviews the senseless killing of Mr. Krentz while was working on his 35,000 acre ranch. The apparent killers were tracked to the Mexican border where they crossed He covered other problems related to border lawlessness.

Articles that show the criminal element problems that illegal marijuana creates:

- *Wall Street Journal*, February 21 and 22, 2009 by David Luhnow and Jose De Cordoba "The Perilous State Of Mexico."

- *Wall Street Journal* article of February 23, 2009 by Fernando Henrique Cardoso (former president of Brazil), Cesar Gaviria (former president of Columbia) and Ernesto Zedillo (former president of Mexico), "The War on Drugs is a Failure"

- Stephanie Simon article in the *Wall Street Journal* article, "Pot 'Plantations' on the Rise."

- The *Wall Street Journal* article of April 10 and 11, 2010 by Leo W. Banks of Cross Country "Our Lawless American Border."

Peter J. Wallison in the December 30, 2009 *Wall Street Journal* reported that: Edward Pinto, former credit officers for Fannie Mae, and a housing expert researched the condition of Freddie and Fannie's loan portfolio, has found that from time to time Fannie and Freddie began buying risky loans as early as 1993, they routinely misrepresented the mortgages they were acquiring. They reported them as prime when they had characteristic that made them clearly subprime Alt-AA subprime mortgage refers to the credit of the borrower. A FICO score of less than 660 is the dividing line between prime and subprime. According to Mr. Pinto Fannie admitted this in a 3rd quarter 10-Q report in 2008 so the risky practice coincides with direction from HUS's new rules.

Most of the damage was done from 2005 through 2007, during which Congressman Frank said there was no cause for concern. In fact, he said we should roll the dice on subsidized affordable housing. This is according to the May 2009 edition of *Citizen*, where they chronicled his support of the finances of Fannie.

- 2000: Concerns about Fannie and Freddie are overblown and there is no federal liability for these two concerns.

- 2002: I don't regard Fannie Mae and Freddie Mac as a problem. I regard them as a great asset.

- 2003: These two entities—Fannie Mae and Freddie Mac—are not facing any kind of financial crisis. The more people exaggerate these problems, the more pressure there is on these companies, the less we will see in affordable housing.

- 2003: I believe there has been more alarm raised about potential unsafely and unsoundness than, in fact exists.

- 2003: There is no federal guarantee of Freddie and Fannie.

- 2003: I don't think we are creating any kind of a crisis.

- 2003: Fannie and Freddie pose no threat to the Treasury, suggesting such could be a self fulfilling prophecy.

Peter J. Allison's article "Fannie and Freddie Amnesia" in the April 20, 2010 *Wall Street Journal*, relates about the July of 2005 when the Senate Banking Committees adopted tough regulatory language on GSEs on a party line vote all Republicans in favor all Democrats opposed. The bill would have established new regulations for Freddie and Fannie requiring them to maintain adequate capital, properly manage their interest rate risk, have adequate liquidity and reserves, and control their asset and investment portfolio growth. He goes on to say there was no action on the Senate bill as it was filibustered and the Republicans had only 55 votes and needed 5 Democrats to support the bill. Out of 45 members of the Democrats caucus, which included Barak Obama and Chris Dodd, they could not get any Democrats to support the bill.

Mr. Williams opines that the date of the bill was important. If legislation along the lines of the Senate Committee bill had been enacted that many of the losses Fannie and Freddie, have or will suffer, might have been avoided.

Edward Pinto's article from the *Wall Street Journal* on November 2009 is quoted as follows: "The goal of the community groups was to force Freddie and Fannie to lower its credit standards." Thus a provision was inserted in the law whereby Congress signaled the GSE's that they should accept down payments of 5% or less, ignore impaired credit over one year old and otherwise ignore their lending guidelines." As a result of congressional and regulatory action the percentage of mortgages, not guaranteed rose with 5% or less down rose from 9% in 1991 to 27% in 1996 reaching 29% in 2007

The source for "Freddie and Fannie" was subject to "affordable housing" regulations issued by HUD, which required them to buy mortgages made by homeowners below the median income. In :Citizen, May 2009" they reported that HUD gave Fannie and F reddie specific targets – 42% of their mortgage financing had to go to borrowers with income below the medium for their area. The target increased to 50% in 2000 and 52% in 2005.

The source for the statistic: "This quota began at 30% in the early 1990's and gradually increased to 52% by 2005" is November 13 2009 *Wall Street Journal*, Edward Pinto and March 2009 citizen.

The *Wall Street Journal* article of December 14, 2009 relates to an interview with Paul Volker. The article entitled "Paul Volker Think more Boldly" was the resource for his comments. The Chairman asked, "Does financial innovation contribute to growth?" He opined that the only financial innovation that improved society was the ATM.

Kate Kelly's *Wall Street Journal* article of January 15, 2009 quotes Paul Volcker: "Banks that blend high risk trading with traditional consumer lending face unmanageable conflict of interest and should be broken up."

According to Michael R. Crittenden and Marshall Eckblad's *Wall Street Journal* article "Lending Falls at a Record Pace," initiatives such as the Obama administration's $30 billon small business lending program rely on banks making loans at a time when many of these same banks are struggling with a rising tide of commercial real estate problems. At the same time they are being told to add to their reserves by bank regulators.

According to Sudeep Reddy's May 4, 2010 article "Lending Standards Stay Tight at Banks in the U.S.," "Many U.S. Banks keep credit tight in the first three months of the year." One customer relied on credit lines of $150,000.00, but when the interest rate went up 35% she vowed to never let the banks do that again and is working on reducing debt.

Sara Wallace reports in the *Wall Street Journal* article of June 29, 2010 on the financial bill. In her "The End of Community Banking" she says that "First Federal lends to creditworthy folks who for decades have been well served by bankers who understand their market and can think creatively to structure credit appropriately. It is what community bankers do. Going forward we will no longer be able to evaluate loan applications based solely on the credit worthiness of the borrower. We will be making regulations compliance decisions instead of credit decisions."

In the author's opinion, this will further throttle the small businesses from prospering. For a dramatization of the difference, the movie "It's a Wonderful Life" portrays two bankers, one that considers the capabilities of the borrower in addition to financial factors, like Jimmy Stewart, and one who only looks at the financial factors and collateral of the loan, as Lionel Barrymore portrayed.

From the *Wall Street Journal* Opinion dated June 6-7, 2009 "Worse than Fiction": The Annan report cities Hurricane Katrina as a case studying the economic consequences of climate change. Yet there's not even remotely conclusive evidence that temperature increases have any effect on the intensity or frequency of hurricanes.

The *Wall Street Journal* article of January 23-24, 2010: "The IPCC, whose 2007 report insisted the glaciers, which feed the rivers that in turn feed much of South Asia, were very likely to disappear by the year 2035. It turns out this prediction was taken from a report of The World Wildlife Fund. It was based on a comment by Indian glacier expert Syed Hasnain from 1999. Mr. Hasnian now says he was misquoted.

The *Wall Street Journal* article November 28, 2009 "Review & Outlook" "Rigging a Climate Consensus"

The *Wall Street Journal* article of November 23, 2009 by Keith Johnson:" Climate Strife Comes to Light "some e-mails also refer to efforts by scientists who believe man causing global warming to exclude contrary views from important scientific publication.

Richard S. Lindzen wrote in the *Wall Street Journal* article of December 1, 2009 entitled "The Climate Science Isn't Settled": The general support for global warming is not in the quality of the data but that there was a little ice age from about the 15th to the 19th century. Thus it is not surprising that temperatures should increase as we emerged from this episode. This happened to coincide with the industrial revolution with increasing emissions of carbon dioxide.

Jeffrey Ball's *Wall Street Journal* article "The Earth Cools, and Fight over Warming Heats Up" includes an accompanying graph showing recent cooling. None of the global warming advocates predicted this cooling.

1. Data from George Will's April 10, 2010 article in News Week "This Nuclear Option is Nuclear."

2. Recently reported in the *Wall Street Journal*.

3. The *Wall Street Journal* report on Energy February 22, 2010 "The Long Road to An Alternative-Energy Future" page R-5 Solar.

4. Yulita Chernova. May 10, 2010 *Wall Street Journal* article "Getting Smart About Smart Meters" and "Electricity: The New Math" Rebecca Smith's article in the *Wall Street Journal* February 19,2010.

5. Robert Bryce's *Wall Street Journal* article of March 5, 2009 "Let's Get Real About Renewable Energy."

6. Lamar Alexander's article Energy Sprawl and the Green Economy.

Mr. Bryce's *Wall Street Journal* Article in the opinion space of March 5, 2009 gives insight into "Let's Get Real about Renewable Energy." Some of the following quotes are from his article. Hydro Power provides about 2.4% of energy needs. Since 1999 more dams have been removed than built. During this period, 200 dams have been removed. Hydropower produces 16 times more energy than wind and solar. The latest data from the U.S. Energy Administration shows that solar and wind output for 2008 will likely be about 45.493,000 megawatt hours. During the rolling 12 month period ending November 2008, 4,118,198,000 megawatt hours watt hours were generated, about 1.1% from wind and solar.

Lamar Alexander recently outlined in an article "Energy Sprawl and the Green Economy" Ken Salazar's announced plans to cover 1000 square miles of land in Nebraska, Colorado, New Mexico and Utah with solar to collect electricity. Solar collectors need to be washed down once a month or they collect too much dirt to be effective. They must also be cooled by water. Where amid the desert and scrubland will we get the water? Salazar is talking about generating 20% of energy from wind. This would require 186,000, fifty-story windmills which would require an area the size of Virginia Lamar fears we are going to destroy the environment in the name of saving the environment. He opines that "renewable energy is not a free lunch. It is an unprecedented assault on the American landscape . . . . Before we find ourselves engulfed in energy sprawl it is imperative we take a closer look at nuclear power."Lamar's article doesn't mention the massive bird killing from these large generators. It's also interesting that Salazar's proposed construction is always away from the electoral base of the Eastern Democrats. Concurrent with Ken Salazar's pursuit of green energy with higher prices, loss of jobs, problems in quantity production, coupled without aggressive nuclear construction while shutting down the oil production in the gulf is a recipe for critical shortage of electricity.

www.ingramcontent.com/pod-product-compliance
Lightning Source LLC
Chambersburg PA
CBHW031241280526
45784CB00004B/1674